The Earth Of
writing through a time of rupture

arts
letters &
numbers

The Earth Of: Writing Through a Time of Rupture

Published under the direction of Arts Letters & Numbers, Averill Park, NY

ISBN: 978-1-71655-919-8

Design by Christine Lorenz in collaboration with the authors

Arts Letters & Numbers
1523 Burden Lake Rd. Averill Park, NY 12018

www.artslettersandnumbers.com

The Earth Of

The Earth of ...

object lessons (3) –– 115

(coda) —–179

Note::
Photographs, graphics, and other visuals not otherwise cited are intended by their respective authors to function as part of the texts they accompany, and are copyrighted by those authors

The Earth of...

Foreword
The Earth Of: Between Hope and Despair
David Gersten

> For a poet's despair in not just personal; he despairs of the word and that implicates all our hopes. Every time a poet writes a poem, he is asking the question, do words hold good? And the answer has to be yes: it is the contra-factual condition upon which a poet's life depends.[1]
>
> *Anne Carson*

The Earth Of begins deep within this contra-factual condition implicating all of our hopes, the Earth of root, of source, a flint stone sparking rising fires, a fragile ground providing structure, the Earth of us, containing us, moving through us, including us, allowing the rolling motion of the human condition to work into our life / words binding the strength of fragility, the fragility of strength. Heard in their own proper beat and measure, these works offer a deeply human sonnet whispering in gentle overtones and roaring howls. Each voice itself contains a constellation of life words empathetically calling us close, revealing heights, depths and fragile grounds.

A story can be 'of' something, but it always 'is' something; listening to our stories is directly linked to our capacity to listen to the world. *The Earth Of* contains the capacity to at once situate our individual imaginations and construct shared stories between us, binding together our humanity. The stories between us, between us and our works, between us and each other, may constitute that displaced place we call home. An authorship grounded in *The Earth Of* may ultimately have the capacity to construct a multitude of living stories that at once shelter the life of our personal imagination and constitute a social contract, a shared story, written with all the nuance and imagination of life itself.

This publication presents a rare intelligence, capturing and embodying with great nuance, a unique period in our lives. The precision and emotive power of the works documented here calls for slow absorption, for considered time, for a deliberate unplugging from the flood of fragmentary images, word clips, and sound bites that fill our days. These works are gifts of hope and despair; they invite thoughtful reflection on life, loss and memory within this pause/rupture.

William Burroughs famously said that 'language is a virus' and while this has always given me a certain pause, in fact a chill, I imagine, that if this is true, language is an airborne virus. Words have an inside/outside life of their own, breathing in and out, moving within us and between us, at once, binding our individual

---

1   Anne Carson, "Economy of the Unlost", *All Candled Things*. (Princeton University press, 1999), p.121

thoughts and our shared stories, positioning language as one of the foundations of our individual being and our civilization. We breath words, they enter us, they are participants in our thoughts and actions, opening the possibility of a communicative exchange between our inner being and our shared stories.

> With its seemingly unlimited growth of material power, mankind finds itself in the situation of a skipper who has his boat built of such a heavy concentration of iron and steel, that the boats compass points constantly at herself and not north. With a boat of that kind no destination can be reached; she will go around in a circle, exposed to the hazards of the winds and the waves.[2]
>
> *Werner Heisenberg*

Perhaps the world is broken, fractured, fragmented, as much of the confusion, crisis and brutality of the 20th and now 21st century would seem to prove. Perhaps as much of late 20th century philosophy sought to prove, we are destined to forever drift within fragmentary shards of meaning, leaving the Earth walled off, trapped, abandoned in irreconcilable difference. Or perhaps, all of this will be eclipsed by an act of nature or an act of will.

> Every epoch is a sphinx which plunges into the abyss as soon as its riddle is solved. [3]
>
> *Heinrich Heine*

I believe *The Earth Of* contains a riddle, contains our best hope against self-destruction, our best hope of finding north. The poetic imagination is perhaps the most pragmatic means of addressing our social and political lives. It affords a means of comprehending this fragile globe, and its people, it produces oxygen within the fibers of our social contract, pockets of words within the collapsed structure of capitals hegemonic language, the poetic imagination is a dimension of human life, a mode of insurgency, a countering of entropy, a language of empathy and difference that includes our nuanced fragilities, in our shared stories. If we are to address our global crisis, perhaps we must begin in recognizing that our lives and our words are structurally bound, that between hope and despair, the Earth of is the contra-factual condition upon which our lives depend. As we struggle to find a largeness of being that survives the prism of capital our world is becoming, perhaps the greatest source of this largeness of being is found in the fragility of

2   W. Heisenberg, "Rationality in Science and Society", *Can We Survive Our Future?* (Bodely Head, 1971), p.84
3   Heinrich Heine, *The Prose Writings of Heinrich Heine* (Walter Scott, 1887), p. 71

being. For in the act of recognizing fragility, ethics finds its meaning, and ethical practice becomes significant.

I am deeply moved by the precision and emotive depth of these works and the people who participated in this workshop. I want to thank Ginger Teppner from the bottom of my heart, for sharing her gifts as a remarkable teacher and for having the generosity of spirit, care and courage, to lead this project in these challenging times. I believe that exploratory, independent, uncontainable works spark from the pragmatics of the poetic imagination in search of the ethical dimensions of life. This publication is bursting with the many lives of *The Earth Of*.

Preface

The Earth Of...

Ginger Teppner

When it became clear that ALN was not going to be able to hold in person work-shops over the summer due to the pandemic, David and Frida asked me if I would be willing to attempt to translate what would have been a week-long residency on site into a virtual experience. Collectively, humanity had crossed a threshold of such significant intensity it manifested as rupture. Reality at once burst so suddenly and completely required a new manner of discourse, a new approach to the page: fresh eyes. While we were quietly skeptical, we hoped to alchemize the embodied experience and to facilitate emotional interchange and engagement that might mirror in person physical proximity of difference. The Earth Of started as an experiment: an investigation of what might be possible when artists listen beyond the veneer of separation, pause, and reconsider all manner of barriers between us as nothing more than mist.

Of course, the pandemic was not our only crisis to contend with. Simultaneously, we were faced with fissures in our fledgling democracy and pressed to recognize our various roles and levels of complicitness, which allowed these cracks to spread towards shattering. The unspoken question: what does it mean to make art when the world is on the cusp? In developing this course I did not explicitly reference the three headed horseman we were facing. I did not want the work created to be about these issues, rather, I hoped for work implicitly *inhabited* by these issues. A body knows what a body knows.

We began the course writing about memories. Memories represent a continuing relationship. We hold specific, detailed, individualized, and filtered memories of places we call home, transformational moments, people we have given love to or received love from, enemies, our bodies, objects that link us to another time, and dreams that reflect the possible significance of what we choose to remember. Like all relationships, the memory relationship deserves and demands to be nurtured, but sometimes all that remains of a memory is a fragment tossed to the birds in the garden, and this ridiculous remainder must somehow suffice. Consider a lingering memory. Write the forbidden. Write the unknown. By this reasoning sometimes a lie is the most honest choice. A lie by another name might represent something once lost that resurfaces as something else re-opens. Clarice Lispector writes, "I know lots of things I've never seen. And so do you. You can't show proof of the truest thing of all, all you can do is believe. Weep and believe." Marguerite Duras describes writing as the pace of words as they pass through a body. Imagine all the ways the memories held within flesh of my flesh, bone of my bone can affect viscosity of language.

The second week further investigated the abstract dance between the internal and external connected by breath as introduced in Charles Olsen's manifesto "Projective Verse" (Juliana Sparh's work offers another exquisite example of this relationship) and the literal dance choreographed by two friends: James Baldwin and William Styron. I wanted the participants to experience catharsis through connection to the reader— to heal by discovering or exposing community where no established language allowed community before. We also further explored the dance between content and form. The writing prompt was to compose a prose poem that incorporated at least one piece of factual information. It could be a scientific fact or an emotional fact. I asked the writers to pick a fact that weaved information and images, which pushed up against each other. Mallarme says "… the intersections, the crossing of the unexpected with the known…" are what causes meaning and not just the facts on their own. I asked them to start concrete, and as they progressed, dive more and more into the abstract. I hoped they would keep in mind the dance inherent in language. How combustion is a chain reaction and once started, a fire produces its own heat.

The last two weeks focused on vulnerability and integrity. To take full responsibility for the framework of one's life necessitates these attributes. To be vulnerable and integrous are revolutionary acts. All writing is political if politics involves (defined by language) specific choice. I wanted the writers to lean into "pure persuasion" without judgment as being more effective than writing that "inflicts" moral authority— inflict being a political choice steeped in rhetorical language. To be vulnerable and integrous demands discernment. I reject the notion of vulnerability as weakness. To the contrary, to be a fluid connector, an intermediary, warrants strength of character. To join the open and closed (hinge), to reflect/see (mirror) and to obscure blindly or with intention (eclipse), even temporarily, requires cohesion and sincerity. All writers are capable of wounding and being wounded. To be a writer warrants strength of character. To be a writer requires being uncomfortable, accepting the paradoxical, and swimming in the rupture.

To name violence, to specifically acknowledge its various inherent manifestations is the beginning of allowance, which leads to the possibility of creating a permeable open space, a border space, a connecting space. What we refuse to see, to look straight in the eye, festers. Festering eventually leads to eruption. Poetry resides in these fissures. The poet then the facilitator, healer, synapse, filter.

To see, does not demand the see-er never look away. I believe it is necessary to be aware of the named but not to obsess it into perpetuity. What I mean is there is a difference between forgetfulness and memory loss. Even if one actively forgets in order to allow the healing space to open, the memory resides. When I suggest it's time to move past the case history, I am in no way suggesting an erasure of memory, only that if one is begging for unity, some violence must be relinquished—recognized and released. It stands to reason this act needs to be resolved on an individual basis in order to address the greater human dissonance. The cliché still resonates: heal yourself— heal the world. In other words: recognize the violence in yourself as an equivalent fraction of world scale violence, recognize, forgive oneself one's perfect imperfection, allow the healing space to open, fill first the boundary space with words and breath, watch what stories spill across containment borders. Connect. Breathe. Connect. Breathe. Connect. Heal.

Maggie Nelson begins *Bluets*: "Suppose I were to begin by saying that I had fallen in love with a color. Suppose I were to speak this as though it were a confession; suppose I shredded my napkin as I spoke." She continues for 95 pages to refract personal suffering and the limitations of vision and love through blue. All things equal, the simplest choice is often the best and through simplicity, "choice" is sometimes able to slip unnoticed through the back door where "allowed," even by accident to resonate, it reaches a predestined audience of one...sometimes one ear hears for an entire population and in this manner work can reach a larger audience. I asked the participants to pick something to fall in love with, to write about this something every day, perhaps multiple times a day, with new eyes. Every warp of canvas under a microscope for long enough falls into perfect inevitable time.

It was an honor to BE with this incredibly gifted and accomplished group of artists. I watched as they worked through the craft and process and pedagogy and style and voice of a diverse spectrum of authors ranging from M. Norbese Phillips to Gertrude Stein to Barbara Guest to Akilah Oliver to Jack Collom to Amiri Baraka to Cecilia Vicuna. What emerged in their responses to the writing, both in their own work and the group discussions was astonishing. There is no question that the crises we face as a global nation inhabited this experience. The writer will write the unsaid whether they realize this or not. There is also no question, that under the right set of circumstances, the virtual geography we have been forced to inhabit, that we presume splits us apart, may also serve to cleave us together. The universal bond of sharing that connects all humanity is alive and well even if we can't physically touch each other or literally inhale each other's breaths as we intently listen and witness this novel shared experience.

I would like to especially share my gratitude for Christine Lorenz who selflessly volunteered to curate this project. Christine, I bow to you. To everyone that was part of this amazing journey and has contributed to this archive of our time together, I borrow words gleaned from Ubuntu Philosophy: I am because you are.

Ginger Teppner 08/03/2020

handing over and passing on, attempting to think our way through

what was once or what will once again.

wayfinding,
place holding

(1)

Blaze Navigation
Tielin Ding

When hiking New York's Harriman State Park in 2019, I became obsessed with the trail markers on the trees and stones. At one point I was running alone in the forest to get a sense of blurring during shooting images on film and started losing my sense of direction. This made me consider the question: where will we go in life? What is the next step? I picked up these trail markers in my memory and practiced them in Massachusetts. It became a way to explore indeterminacy, and legibility or illegibility, when it was brought out of its original context and put into another public space as a certain kind of communication language. I am planning to apply as a volunteer in the New York-New Jersey Trail Conference, in order to find out how this trail system works within different sites, along with the drifting of trail markers through time and location.

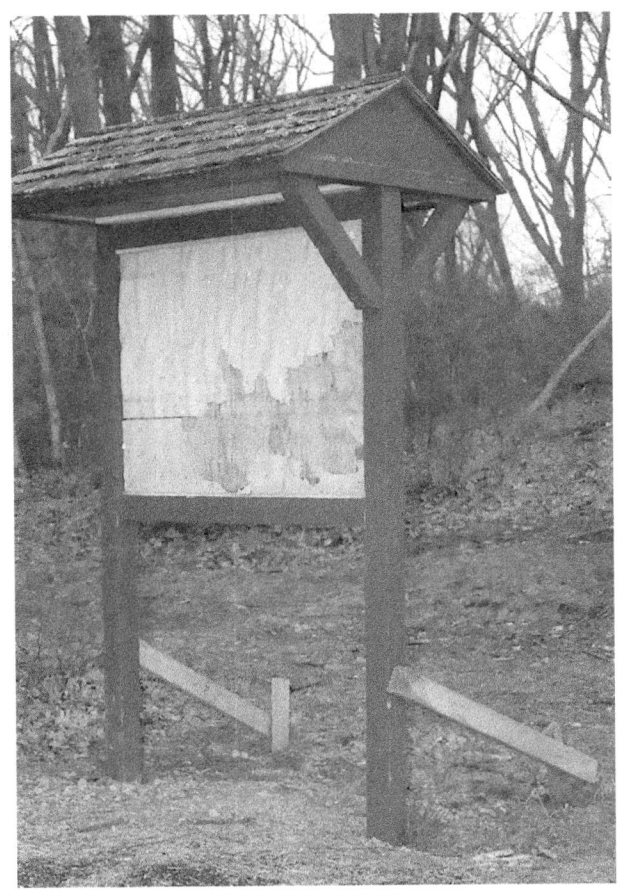

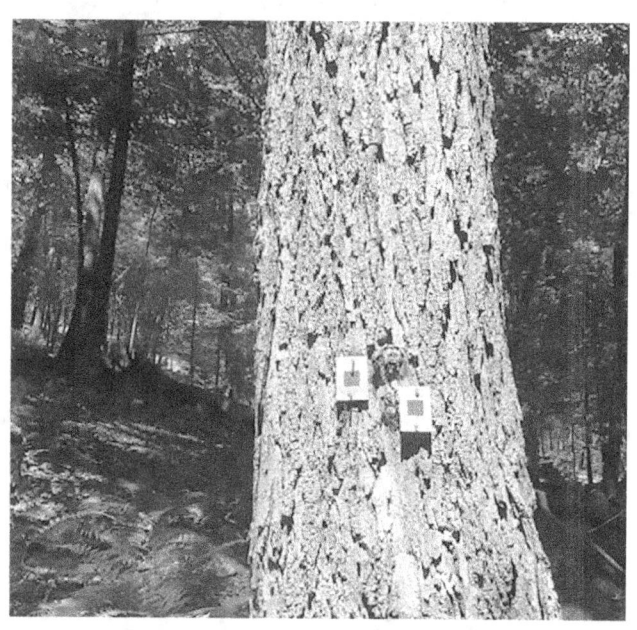

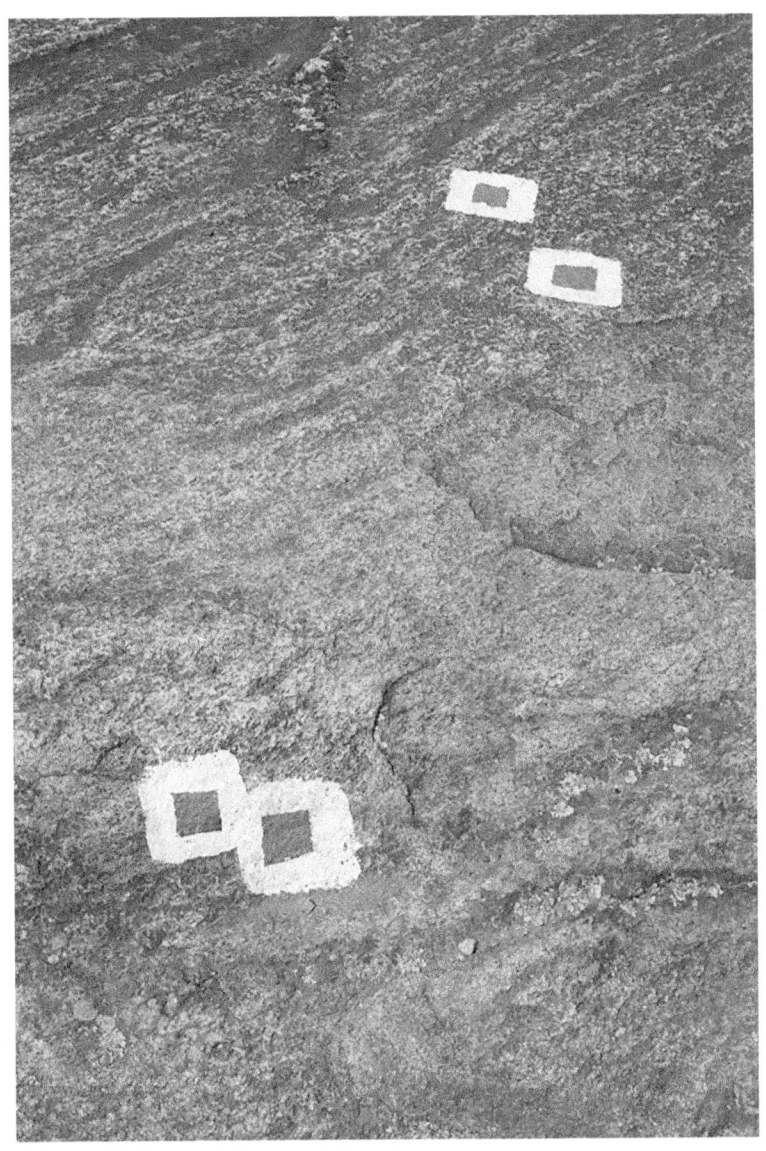

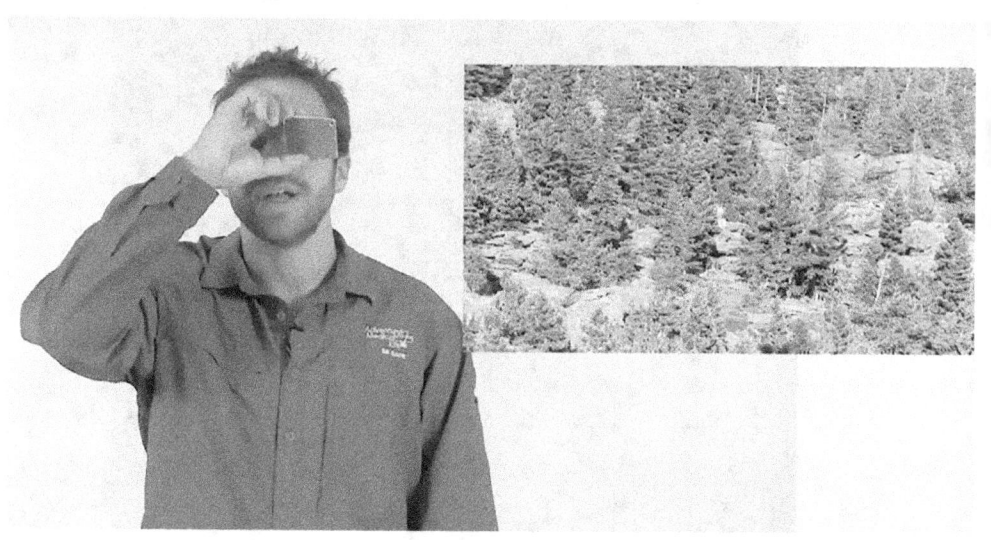

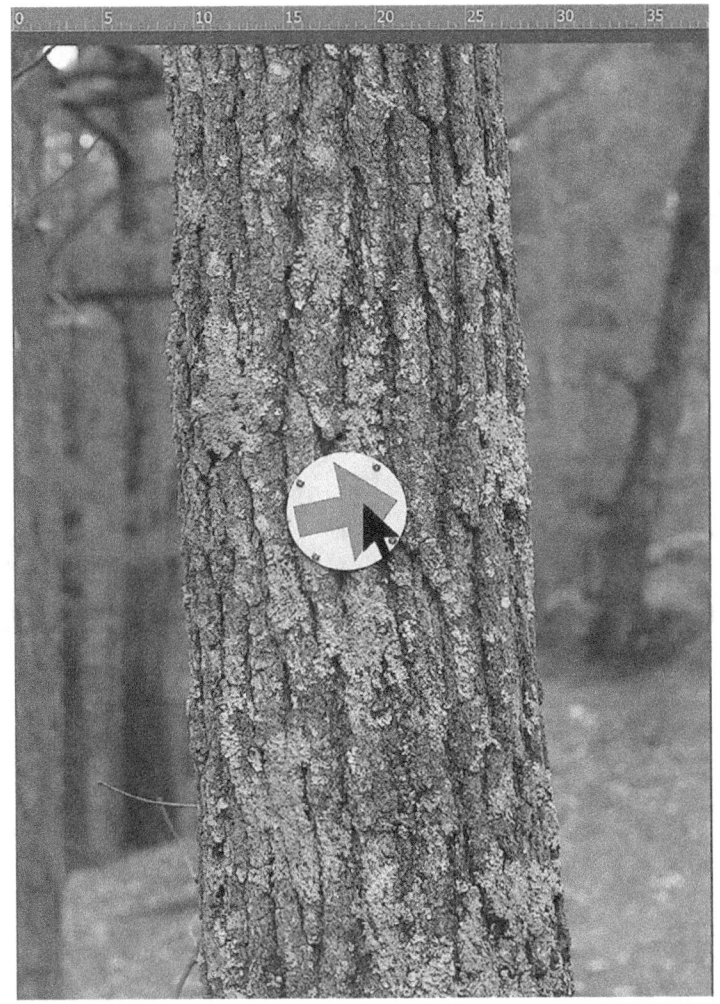

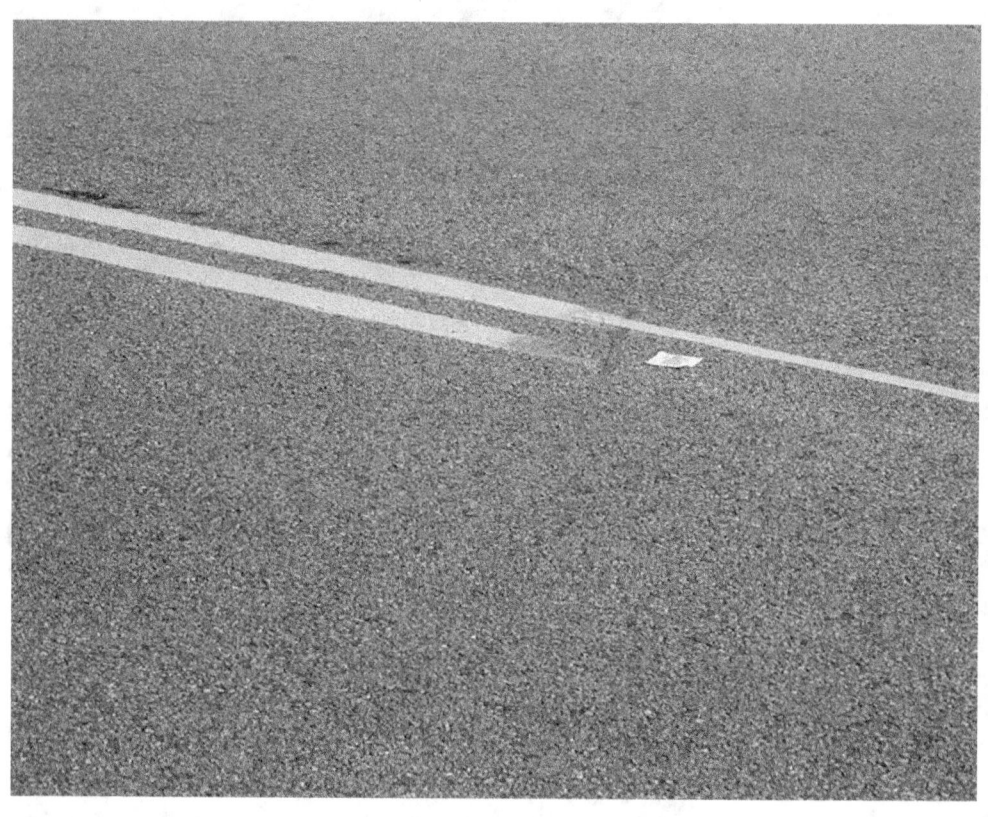

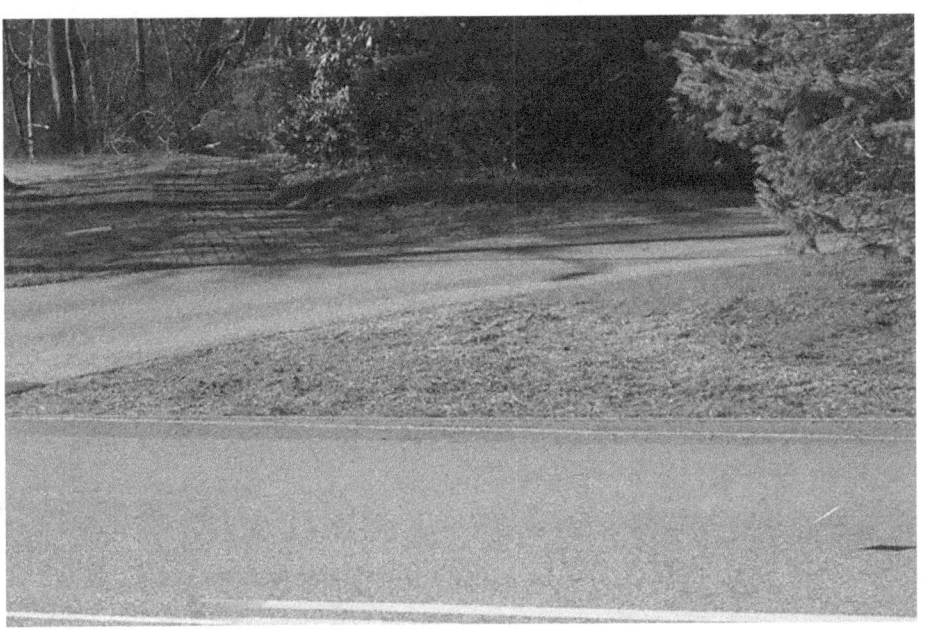

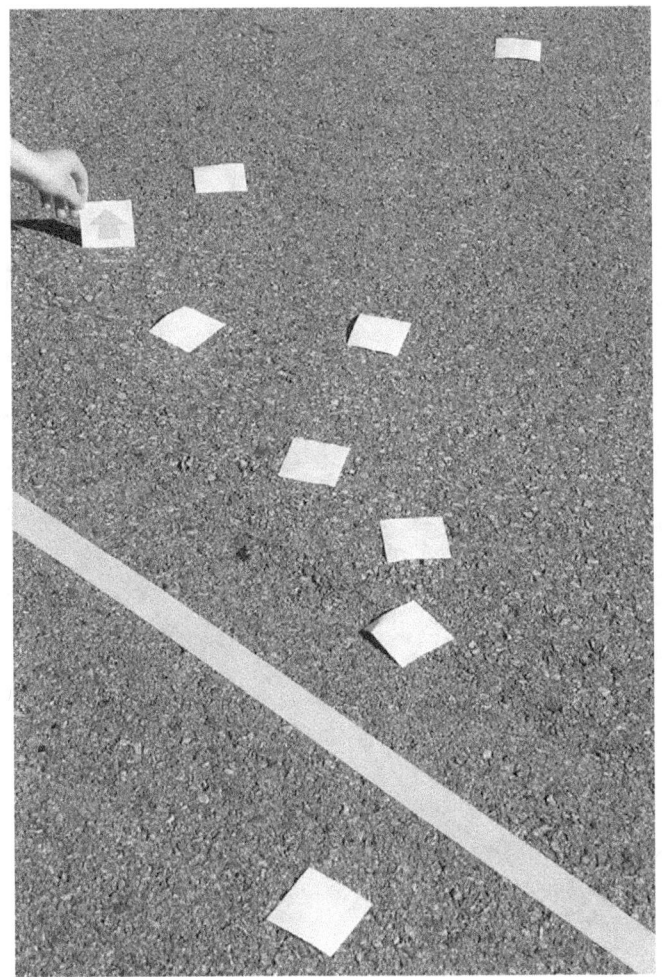

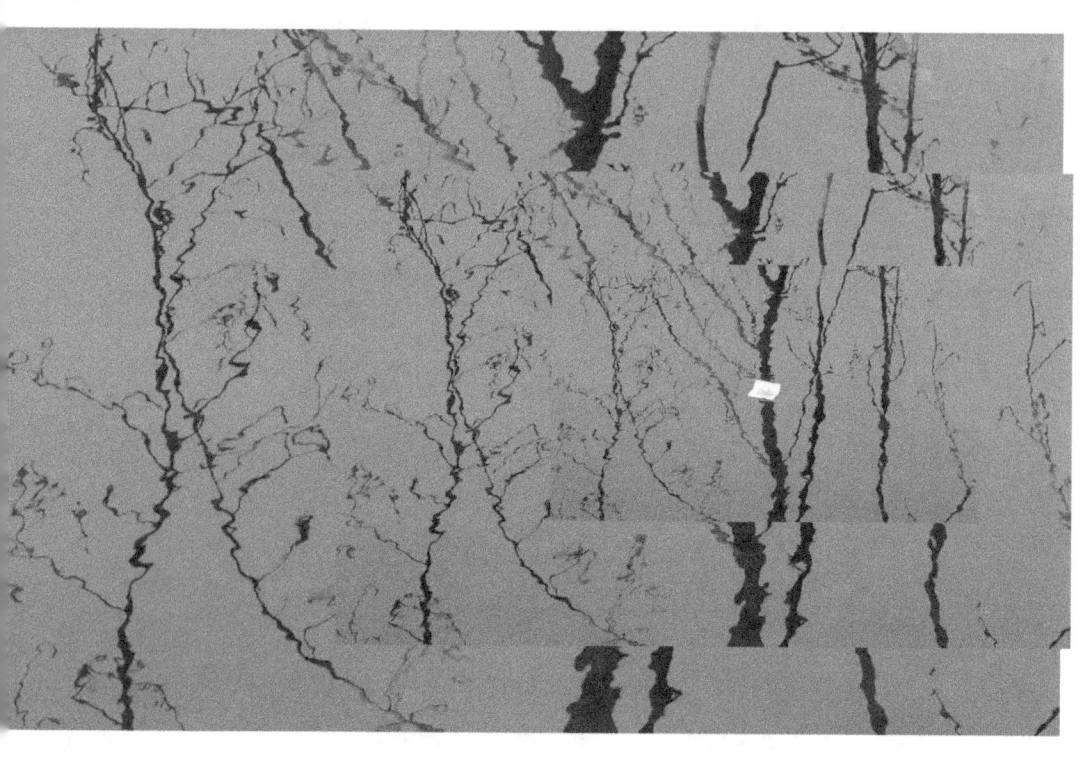

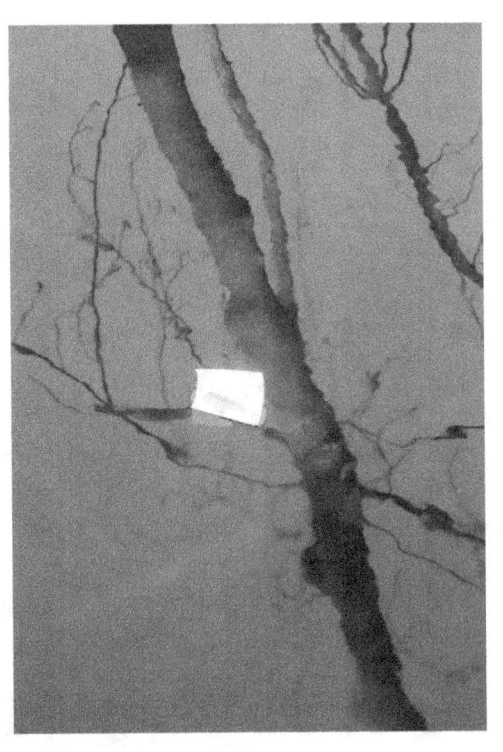

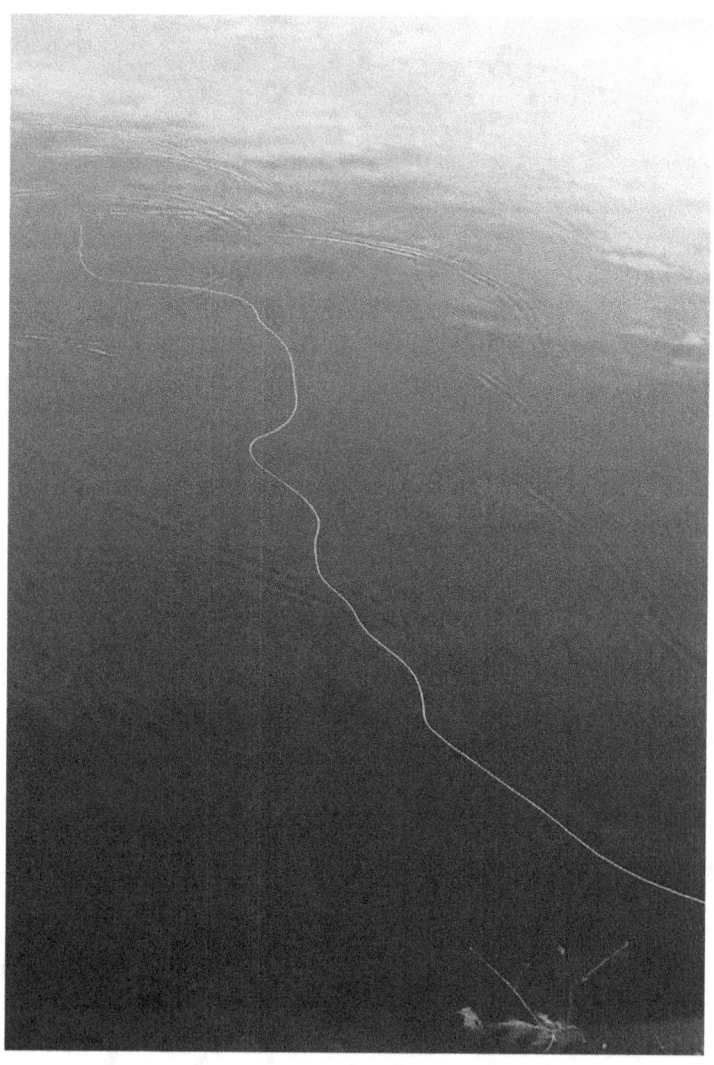

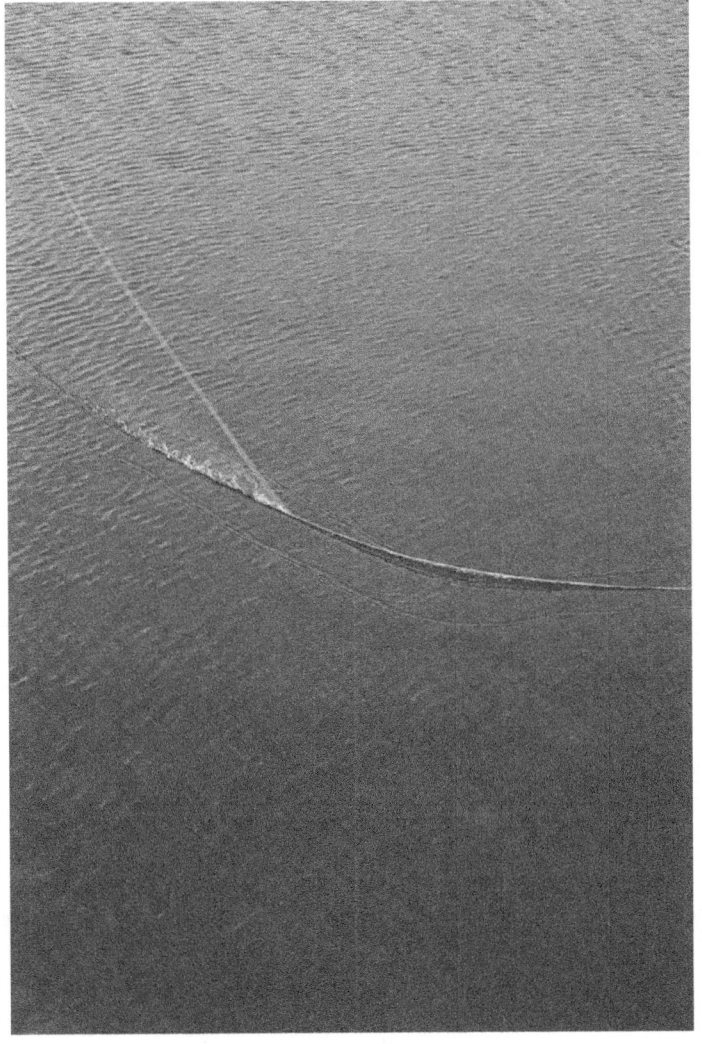

The Mill

Evan Burgess

1. Begin.

Hello!

It's so good to see you here!

There is so much that I want to show you.

I have to run to Hannaford's, but I'll just drop you off here by the Mill.

Please, take a look around!

[[Okay.|Mill Front Lot]]

2. Mill Front Lot

You are standing in the driveway in front of the Mill.

The grass is getting quite long in the field to your right.
To your left, metal steps lead up the side of the mill to
the second floor. Below the steps, a large door leads in to
the first floor of the Mill. And straight ahead, a series of
earthen steps snakes up through a forested hill.

[[Climb the metal stairs to the Mill.|Mill Stairs]]

(if: $BeenInMill is 0)[

Alternatively, you could:

][[Go into the first floor of the Mill.|The Mill Downstairs]]

[[Walk into the field.|The Field]]

[[Climb the earthen steps.|The Earthen Steps]]

(set: $HillLocation to 0)

3. Mill Stairs

You are standing on the metal grille platform at the top of
the stairs to The Mill. A ladder leads up to the roof. Too
dangerous, in my opinion.

(if: $BeenInMill is 0)[The door to the mill is covered in cracked
white paint. A hornet crawls out of a small hole in the door.
Being careful to avoid the hole, you push the door open.] (if:
$BeenInMill is 1)[There is a breeze here. It's nice. It was too
warm in the mill. You look lazily out over the field.

There is a glass dish of cigarette butts at your feet. This is
the place where your mind goes whenever you smell stale cigarette
smoke in the city.

]

[[Enter The Mill|The Mill Upstairs]]

[[Go down to the driveway|Mill Front Lot]]

4. The Mill Upstairs

(set: $BeenInMill to 1)

You are in the Mill.

The [[floorboards|Mill Floorboards]] run diagonally under your feet. The [[barn boards|Mill Rafters]] in the ceiling float lightly overhead, supported by wooden trusses and steel ties. In all directions, windows let in light except where they are removed to let in air.

You are in a single room that must span at least a hundred feet wide and fifty feet deep. Smells of warm pine. Papers are scattered across the floor. Speakers and projectors are pointing at different walls at random. People have been doing work here, and it looks like there is room for you too.

(link: "Look around.")[

You see:

[[A Swing.|Mill Swing]]

[[An Elevator.|Mill Elevator]]

[[A Bathroom.|Mill Bathroom]]

Looking a bit further, you see:

[[A patch of gravel floor, off to the left.|Mill Gravel]]

[[The door to the kitchen, off to the right.|Mill Kitchen]]

]

[[Step outside.|Mill Stairs]]

5. Mill Floorboards

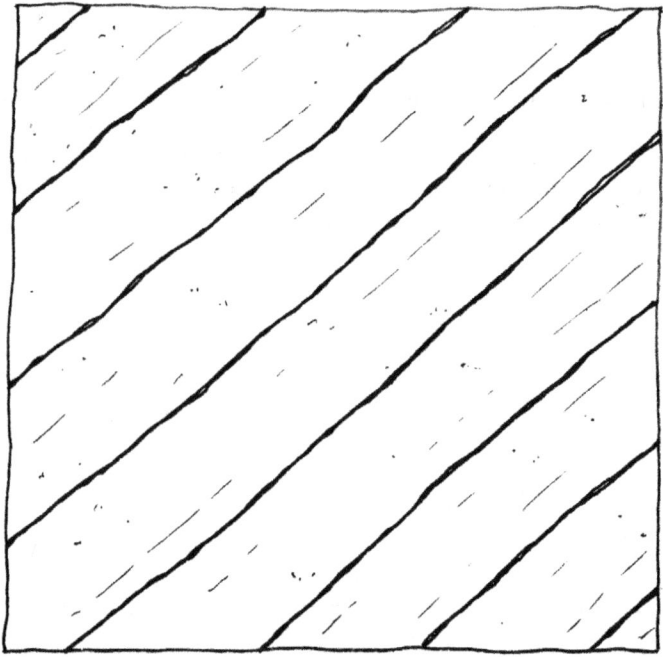

[[Go Back.|The Mill Upstairs]]

6. Mill Rafters

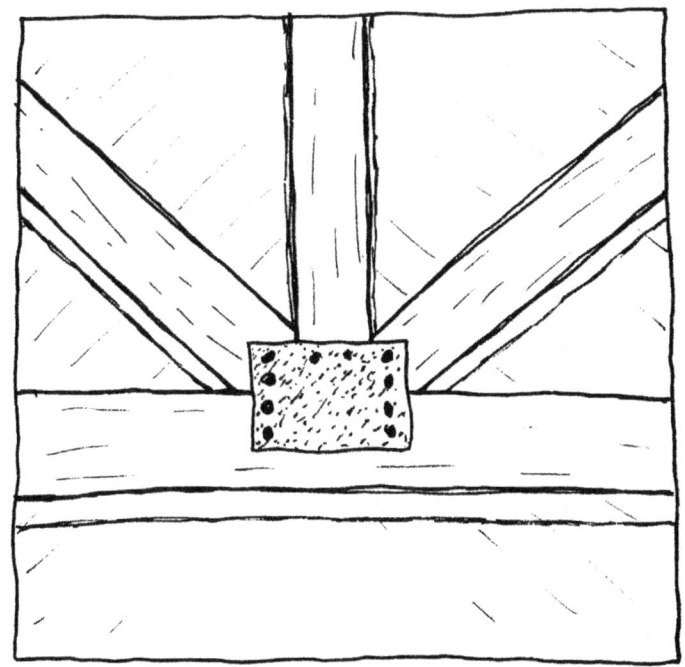

[[Go Back.|The Mill Upstairs]]

7. Mill Swing

A wooden plank swing hangs by long ropes from a sturdy red pipe 30 feet above your head.

(link: "Sit down.")[You sit on the swing. Your feet do not touch the ground. If you pull backward on the ropes, your body pushes forward to center the gravity. You loosen your pull, and your body moved backwards. You are swinging.

You stare straight ahead for a few minutes, then let your eyes wander. Up above, in the corner of the room, there is a nook up by the ceiling. It looks like someone has nailed a few boards into the wall to make a path up to the nook. But an easy path? No. I heard there are bats up there.

Below, there is a platform on wheels. A set of stair to nowhere. And it has wings. Or ears? Surely that's why they call it the Rabbit. Did this come from Hejduk somehow?]

(link: "Stand up.")[You lift yoursef up by the ropes, placing one foot on the swing, then the other. You close you eyes. Extending your arms above your head, you hold the ropes, shifting your weight between your arms and your legs to remind yourself that you are in balance.]

[[Back|The Mill Upstairs]]

8. Mill Elevator

You circle around the standalone bathroom, finding yourself in the back corner by the freight elevator.

A laundry machine runs in the nook next to you.

[[Go Back.|The Mill Upstairs]]

9. Mill Bathroom

You circle around the freestanding bathroom in the back-center
of the Mill. Depending on the day, the door will either not
lock, or permanently lock (please be careful!). It's sizeable
for a bathroom, there's a full shower in addition to the sink and
toilet.

Surely, this bathroom would be free of any constructed optical
curiosities.

Nope. No it is not. Perhaps you would like to investigate:

(link: "The backwards mirror.")[Two mirrors are installed at
right angles in the corner of the bathroom. As you look into the
corner, they appear to be four mirrors forming a cross. And,
directly across from you, you see yourself looking back. It is
a mirror, after all. But the intersection between the two mirors
stays planted firmly at the location of your pupils, no matter
what angle you look from.

Most mirrors will mirror your image. This one does not.]

(link: "The Camera Obscura")[Most bathrooms do not have holes
installed in the walls. This is not most bathrooms. A square
tunnel, large enough to comfortably reach an arm through, is cut
and framed into the wall between you and the main work space. A
tiny door is installed at each end of the tunnel for privacy. and
between the two doors are a series of lenses that can slide in and
out of the tunnel.

The bathroom is the body of a camera. If there is light in the
Mill, and darkness in the Bathroom, and a lens in between, the
image of the Mill will be projected, inverted, onto a paper hung
in the bathroom. You can move the paper to focus the image.
Thank you Troels.]

[[Go back.|The Mill Upstairs]]

10. Mill Gravel

At the left most fifth of Mill floor, the floorboards end and you step onto a gravel bed. You kick the gravel beneath your feet, then quickly sweep it back so that it isn't too uneven.

In front of you is a standalone gypsum wall with a loose ink painting on a large sheet of paper.

Behind of you is a black table housing a grid or square compartments.

You sense that each of these objects as accumulated an enormous amount of care.

(link: "Approach the painting.")[You walk up to the ink painting (drawing?), but you realize that, given its size, it gets harder to see the closer you get. It is a whirlwind of lines and circles.

You have trouble entering the painting, and begin to feel self-conscious. Maybe you'll understand it better later.]

(link: "Walk around the standalone wall.")[Oh. It's the tech closet. So that's where they keep all the broken projectors.]

(link: "Approach the table.")[It's so strange to see it in person. This is the table that David and the rest of his class used as the site for their thesis project. You've heard the story many times, and you know that it holds extra weight after John's passing.]

[[Go Back|The Mill Upstairs]]

11. Mill Kitchen

There is one large wall constructed in the upper floor of the
Mill, separating off the last quarter of the space from the main
area. Passing through a door in the wall, you find yourself in a
smaller but equally bright area as windows continue to line the
perimeter.

Two long tables are set up in here, with enough seating to serve
dinner to fourty people. Bricks are piled up next to an old
wood-burning furnace that used to heat the space. There are old
cabinets that were once used to organize letters for type-setting.

(link: "At the near end of the room, a large kitchen takes up
most of the space.")[You wander around the kitchen area, which
wraps around the end of the room. Counters, sinks, pots and pans
on top of pots and pans, silverware drawers, shelves of cups
and glasses (remember to return your cups!), washing and drying
stations, spice racks, a large refrigerator (Do not touch, dinner
food only!), and a deep freezer chest (sombody remember to refill
the ice trays!). And in the center, a large island with plenty of
space for many hands to help prepare for dinner. A large bag of
fresh vegetables is sitting on the island.

(link: "Get a drink of water.")[You pick out a glass from the
shelf under the counter. It is curved with decorative ridges
down the side. You were hoping for a larger glass, but it doesn't
look like there are any here at the moment. There are some papers
sitting on the freezer chest, so you move them to the kitchen
island and open the freezer. Fortunately, there's a full ice
cube tray at the top of the freezer chest, so you crack the ice
and tease out two ice cubes. You return the tray to the freezer,
close the freezer chest, and return the papers to where you found
them.

You walk over to the sink, and find the small knob on the side
where the filtered water is. Technically you can drink the
regular water too, but it tastes a little bit... hard. The ice
cracks in your glass. You drink the water and then refill your
glass (it is a rather small glass, after all). You drink again
and then dump the remainder of the two ice cubes in the sink. You
walk over to the other sink, where the sponges and dish soap are
kept, and wash out your glass. Shaking off the excess water, you
turn over the glass and return it to the shelf.]

]

(link: "At the far end of the room, a half-wall sections off a small office space behind.")[There is a half-height wall covered in books, which separates the eating area from a small office area behind. You pull one of the books off of the wall. It is a biography of Vaclav Havel. A bench lines the wall, and futons are piled up on the bench. You could sleep here if you wanted to.

[[Walk around the wall to the office|Mill Upstairs Office]]

]

[[Go back out to the main Mill space.|The Mill Upstairs]]

12. Mill Upstairs Office

Hiding behind the wall in the dining area, you find a small office area with another table. Bright as ever because of all the windows. There is a set of plastic drawers, a printer, a few stacks of paper. Someone's laptop is sitting on the table. A cash box is sitting next to the printer. This place almost feels private, as if you wandered into the Teachers' Lounge and you aren't supposed to be here. But there was no door, so no harm in looking. Through a door in the side wall, there is another small bathroom.

[[Go in the bathroom.|Mill Office Bathroom]]

[[Go back to the eating area.|Mill Kitchen]]

13. Mill Office Bathroom

This is another small batheroom, this one with a tall ceiling and a large window. There is a large painting sitting in the bathtub. The flush on the toilet is a little bit loose. Other than that, everything is pretty normal.

[[Go back.|Mill Upstairs Office]]

14. The Mill Downstairs

As you step into the ground floor of the Mill, the cool, slightly damp air is soothing in contrast to the warm day outside. The ground floor would be nearly as light and nearly as open as the upper floor, if it weren't for the dozens of metal palettes rising up thirty feet into the air, forming a labyringth through one half of the space (everything to your right), piled high with construction materials, construction equipment, and every type of auto body contraption tht you've never heard of before. The glass and rust keep this area feeling just slightly less than friendly.

To your left is the machine shop. This mill used to be used for manufacturing underwear for men in the war. But these days, David's family have re-outfitted the space to be more in line with their family business: auto body machining. And scattered throughout are various woodworking instruments as well. Band saws, table saws, pull saws, lathes, sanding belts, drill presses, and walls covered in hand tools. Drawers full of every nut and bolt. Cabinets filled with hardened paints and expired solvents.

Immediately to your left, by the door, are protective masks, goggles, gloves, and ear muffs, in case you'd like to use the shop.

At the far end across from you are the double doors to the back porch.

In the corner, an area is sectioned off with an old kitchen, bathroom, and storage area.

Looking left and right, you could:

(link: "Stroll through the junkyard labyrinth.")[You're certainly not wearing thick-soled work boots, so you keep your eyes firmly on the floor, looking out for upturned nails or broken glass, as you carefully step between the metal frames. You walk past a series of boards, a small front-loader, a whole stack of aging, displaced, windows and doors. It might be nice to repurpose one of these doors for something.

As you make your way to a back corner, you are surrounded by metal frames supporting wooden palettes supporting buckets and boards and half-assembled machinery and half-disassembled furniture. If you cleaned up the floor a little bit and brought a chair over here, it might make a nice nook to be alone.

]

(link: "Stroll through the machine shop.")[You stroll between the
milling machines and the drilling machines and the cross-cutting
and the ripping machines. Each is bolted firmly into the concrete
floor, holding steady against its own potential motion, boasting
thick sheets of painted steel between your hands and their blades.
You run your hand along the curves of the metal, being careful to
respect the aura of danger around each of the blades.

Walking the perimeter of the room, you pick up awls and chisels
at random, rotary pipe cutters and angled steel rulers, screws
and nails and washers and bolts, making sure to return each to the
same place where you found it.]

Or perhaps, looking a bit farther, you could:

[[Go out to the back porch.|Mill Back Porch]]

[[Go into the enclosed kitchen area.|Mill Downstairs Kitchen]]

[[Go outside.|Mill Front Lot]]

15. Mill Back Porch

You are standing on the back porch of the Mill. A short driveway
leads from the street to the porch. The neighbor's house is of
the other side of the driveway. The ground floor of the elevator
exits onto the porch, and beyond it is a series of two outdoor
showers enclosed by tall wooden fences.

The garbage dumpster is back here.

[[Go back in the Mill.|The Mill Downstairs]]

16. Mill Downstairs Kitchen

The back corner of the first floor of the mill is closed off, creating a contained space with a slop sink, industral refrigerator, tables, plenty of shelving, and a small bathroom.

On the other side of the bathroom is a decently sized annex with more shelves, some large HVAC equipment, and a vew large potter's wheels.

If you duck through a small storage room in this annex, you can go back out into the machine shop area.

[[Go back.|The Mill Downstairs]]

|cc1>[Oh.]

|cc2)[Oh no.]

|cc3)[I have to tell you a story about this room.]

|cc4)[It was the night before the first time that I ever saw the mill. I wasn't there.]

|cc5)[Apparently a chipmunk had died and left its body behind somewhere in the Mill.[1]]

|cc6)[And a few people, after much deliberation and seeking the blessing of their peers, set up an operating table in the space behind the kitchen.]

|cc7)[In a way not unlike those old paintings of biology lessons, they dissected the chipmunk, veils over their faces.]

|cc8)[And after it was done, they stored the chipmunk in the industrial refrigerator.]

|cc9)[And only much later, after smelling the chipmunk for quite a while, someone realized that the refrigerator was set to "heat" instead of "cool".]

|cc10)[You should look up the photo of the dissection though. Truly a portal into a different time.]

|cc11)[]

(click: ?cc1)[(show: ?cc2)]

(click: ?cc2)[(show: ?cc3)]

(click: ?cc3)[(show: ?cc4)]

(click: ?cc4)[(show: ?cc5)]

(click: ?cc5)[(show: ?cc6)]

(click: ?cc6)[(show: ?cc7)]

(click: ?cc7)[(show: ?cc8)]

(click: ?cc8)[(show: ?cc9)]

(click: ?cc9)[(show: ?cc10)]

---

1   Frida recalls that it was a groundhog

17. The Field

You step into the tall grass of the field that runs parallel to
the road. There is an ashen fire pit in front of you. A mound of
dirt and gravel sits between the field and the driveway. And next
to the gravel sits [[Rocky, the front-loader|Rocky]].

[[Go back to the driveway.|Mill Front Lot]]

18. Rocky

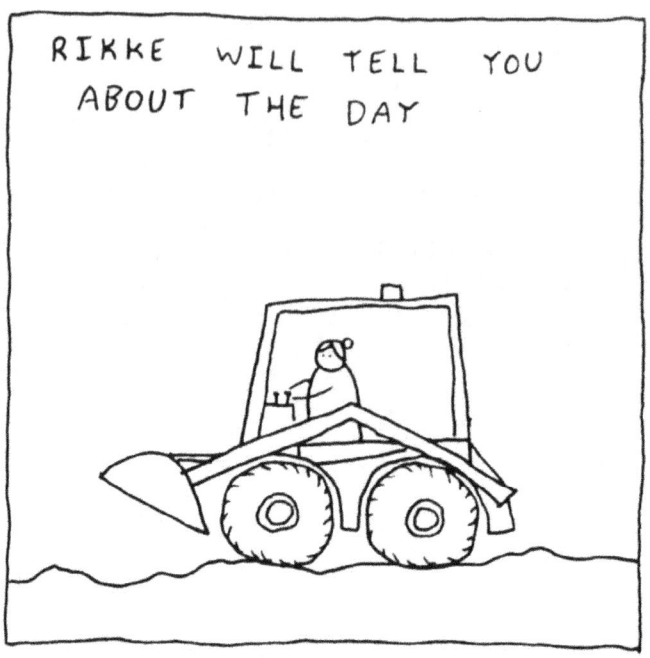

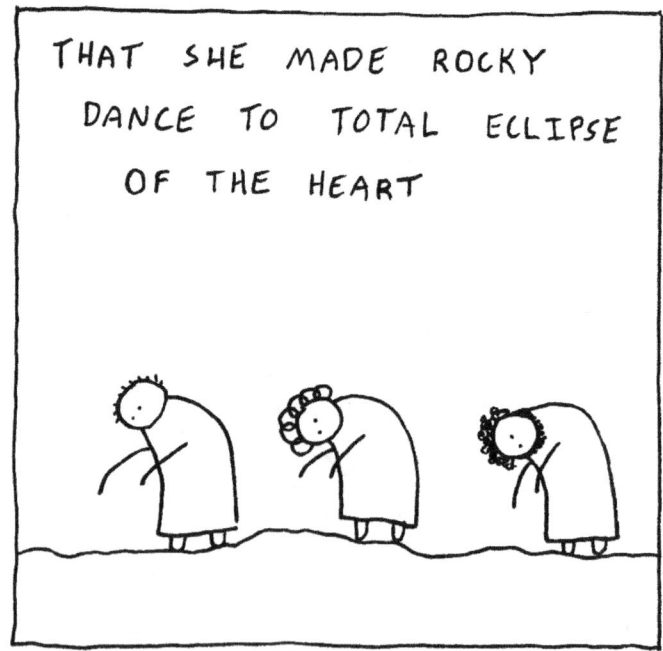

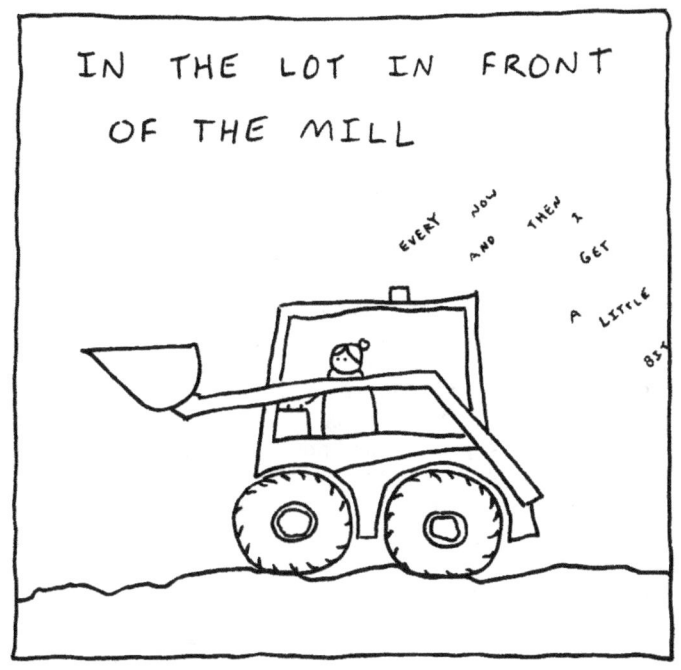

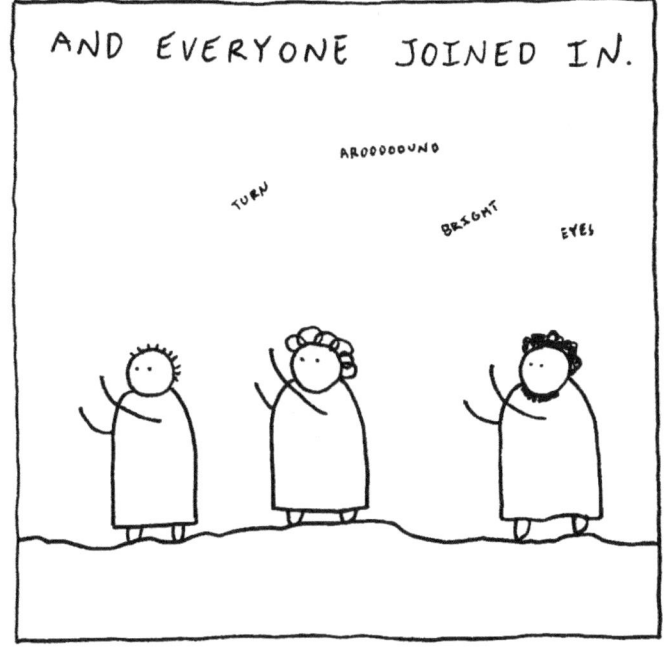

[[Go Back.|The Field]]

19. The Earthen Steps

(if: $HillLocation is 0)[As you climb up the hill, you walk up
a series of steps carved into the earth. Wooden boards make up
the step risers, held in place by wooden stakes driven into the
ground. The boards hold back treads made of gravel and brick
infill, which keeps the steps from flooding during the rain.
The steps are uneven, but they aren't hard to follow.

Avoiding the tall grass on either side of the steps, you use a
few young tree trunks to help pull yourself up the path.](if:
$HillLocation is 1)[As you climb down the hill, you walk down a
series of steps carved into the earth. Wooden boards make up
the step risers, held in place by wooden stakes driven into the
ground. The boards hold back treads made of gravel and brick
infill, which keeps the steps from flooding during the rain.
The steps are uneven, but they aren't hard to follow.

Avoiding the tall grass on either side of the steps, you use a
few young tree trunks to help steady yourself as you make your way
down to the Mill.]

[[Climb up into the Hill|The Hill]]

[[Go down to the driveway in front of the Mill.|Mill Front Lot]]

20. The Hill

You are in the Hill.

You are standing on a flat trail that runs along the center of the Hill. A series of earthen steps leads down to the Mill, and a few additional boards are laid along the path up to the House. The hill is fairly heavily wooded with tall deciduous trees.

If you are not feeling inclined to climb down or up, you could also follow the flat trail along the side of the hill.

[[Walk along the path, away from the street.|The Hill Path]]

(link: "Walk along the path, towards the street.")[Are you wearing your hiking boots? No? Ok, the grass is tall out there. You trek out to a small platform where someone had set up a tent in the past. Yes, they got poison ivy. Come back here before you get it too.]

[[Go down the steps.|The Earthen Steps]]

(set: $HillLocation to 1)

21. The Hill Path

Stepping off the wooden portion of the path, you walk down a short trail that circles the hill. To your left, you can see the Mill through the trees. You are about on the level of the second floor. To your right, looking up the hill, it's harder to make out the House from this angle.

(link: "Step off the path (down).")[

About five feet down and to your left, there a decent sized shelf of flat ground within the hill. You hold on to a tree trunk as you shimmy down to the spot. From here, you can see the side of the mill clearly. Between here and there are layers of weeds and leaves and ivies and a few small trees growing out of the hill. Some corrugated metal is dumped off to the side, and large shrubs block the view between here and the neighbor's property. The only easy way out would be to go back up to the path.]

(link: "Step off the path (up).")[

Realizing that you don't need to stay on the path, you begin to make your way up the hill, weaving between the trees, trying not to slip back down where the ground is steep. You don't need to go too far to satisfy your curiosity. You find a tree to lean against while you look up into the green canopy. A few minutes later, you head back down to the path.]

(link: "Walk to the end of the path.") [

You look down at your feet, and find a smooth rock in the soil.
Carefully prying it out of the earth (it was buried a bit more
than you expected), you wipe it off and hold it in your hand,
by your side. You stroll slowly down the path, planting your
eyes firmly at your feet, making note of all of the other rocks
that you pass on your way. The path takes a short turn, then
ends in a quickly thickening bramble bush. You see at your
feet that someone's been placing rocks at the ground at the
end of the path, though there's still more grass than rock at
present. Plenty of work to do. You place the rock down and go
to find another.]

[[Go back to the steps.|The Hill]]

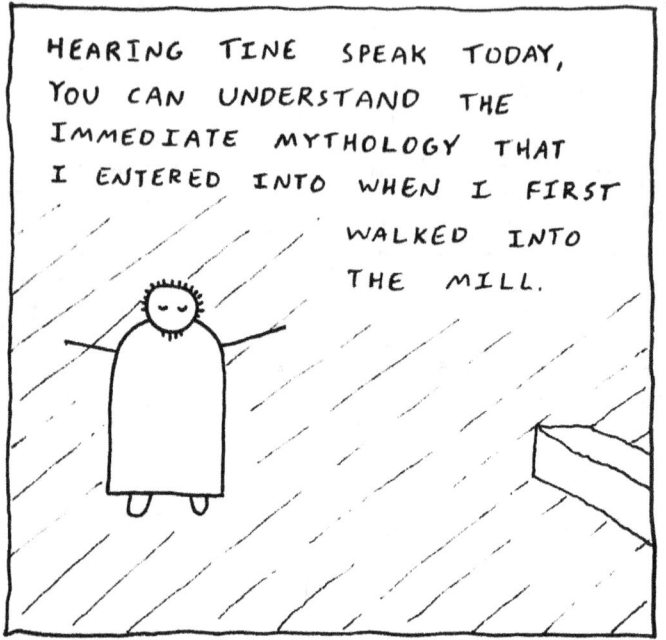

HEARING TINE SPEAK TODAY,
YOU CAN UNDERSTAND THE
IMMEDIATE MYTHOLOGY THAT
I ENTERED INTO WHEN I FIRST
WALKED INTO
THE MILL.

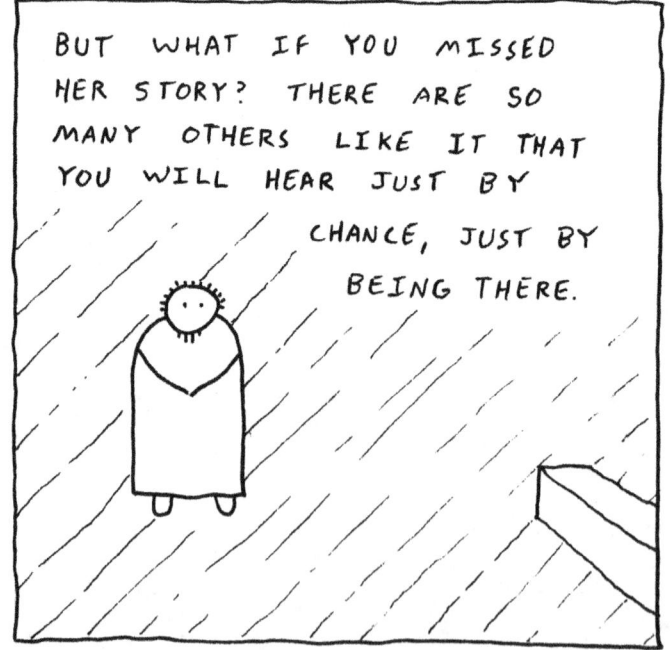

BUT WHAT IF YOU MISSED
HER STORY? THERE ARE SO
MANY OTHERS LIKE IT THAT
YOU WILL HEAR JUST BY
CHANCE, JUST BY
BEING THERE.

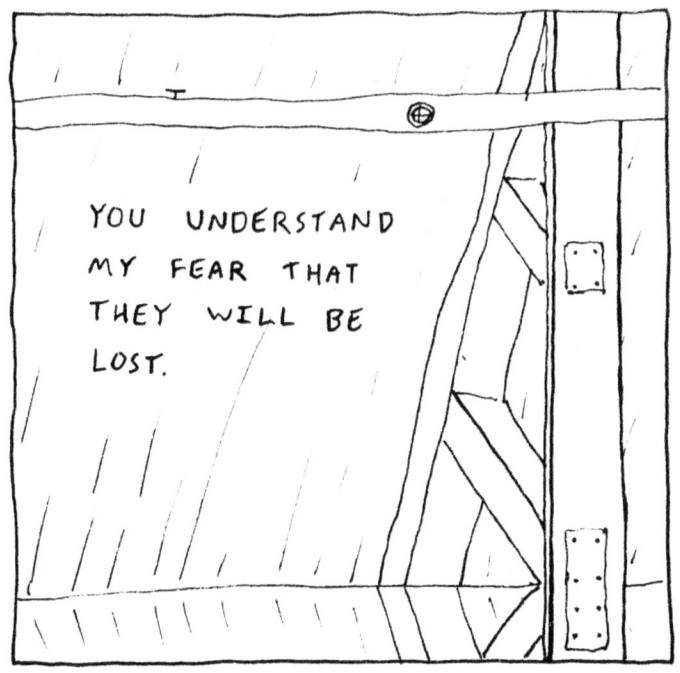

23. Hallway Library

There is a hallway in the house.

There is a library in the hallway.

You are in the library in the hallway in the house.

If this was a classic 1700s New England house, this might be where the enormous brick chimney would sit, with half a dozen fireplaces opening up into every room.

But his house has a central staircase, not a central chimney. And because of an addition to the back of the house, the hallway behind the stair now becomes the center.

On one side is the door to the music room. The door is open. The musicians must not be using it right now. I remember the day when an incredibly kind-hearted opera singer wrote and performed a song in the music room called Goodbye Mill. At the time I don't think I knew whether they were leaving, or whether the Mill was leaving. It turned out to be both, but I know that they'll be back when they can.

On the other side of the hall is the door to the kitchen. It would be unsusal for this door to be closed, as people mill in and out all day. It's late afternoon, so the kitchen is empty. You watch as a fly buzzes in from the back hall, and then out into the kitchen.

On the remaining two sides of the hallway are the threshholds to the front hall and the back hall, but that's just the nature of a hallway.

And in this central hall itself are two bookshelves, one on each side, and an end table in the corner. I've looked through the books on these shelves many times, but I'm not sure that I've ever actually read one. You flip through books of poetry, books on language, books about places, or people, or buildings. You turn around to the other shelf. How were these books organized? I don't remember.

Theres's a small stack of books on the end table. One is a book on sailing. That's probably from Che. Another is a book on loss written by Ira.

It's a nice day out today, so you go about your day. The hallway
isn't designed for spending too much time.

Much later, after dinner, after the lake, after everyone else
is in bed, I pass through the hallway again to look through the
titles of the books. Before long, I find myself wandering into
the kitchen to toast some bread and butter. I can hear Josephine
and Adrianos getting back from the lake, since they stayed out
later. They come in throught the mudroom, through the hallway
library, through the front hall, and up the stairs.

It's late. I should go to bed. I put away the bread and butter and
turn off the lights. There's a switch in the kitchen. There's a
sconce with a pull chain in the music room. And actually, I might
just leave the light on in the hallway in case anyone gets up in
the middle of the night.

Hopkins House Condominium Association

Shou Jie Eng

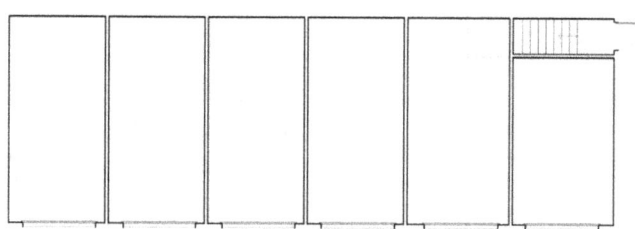

I've been eyeing a carriage house, she tells me, late one night. I see a house in the dark, full of carts, without horses or humans. There is a painter on the second floor who is moving out. He is not there when we first visit, but the space still has his scent. Whites and blues on the plywood floors, paced uncertainly into greys in parts. Tape marks on the walls. Racks, nearly empty, out of two-by-fours with their lumber stamps left on.

❖ ⁘ ❖

Six parking bays   for the five apartments in the main house
a historic house   the John D. Hopkins House
the carriage house   is in the record too
the stair   that leads to the second floor
                        is only accessible from the face
                        invisible from the street.

❖ ⁘ ❖

She wants me to draw up the apartment for her. It will be on the second floor of the carriage house. She wants a large kitchen to cook in, for friends to be with her as she cooks for them. She wants a six-foot tub with a good back, so that she can soak fully, and sit up. She wants to replace the hanging fluorescent work lights. She wants to keep the heavy timber frame. She wants the light from the three p.m. sun to fall on the curve of her back, where her spine dips between her shoulders, on the weekends, when she is at her desk.

❖ ⁘ ❖

There is no gas line to the carriage house. And no hot water heater either. *How did the painter wash his brushes?* I say to no one.

❖ ⁘ ❖

The second floor is not large, which is why it has not sold. I show her two options for a bedroom, given the limited space. She surprises me by asking about flexible living environments. She surprises me by bringing up *critical Italian architecture from the 1960s.* I remember when she used to hate talking about architecture and architects. *You're all so full of shit,* she told me once, in the middle of an argument. *You're full of shit,* she meant. We talk, now, about soft surfaces and bedrooms. The give that a mattress has when you sit down on it, heavily, and let yourself fall backwards in frustration, I want to say but do not.

◆ ✢ ◆

We go back to the carriage house to take measurements. She busies herself with the realtor while I get myself set up. The smell of the painter is nearly gone. She knows that I prefer working in the vacancy of a recently-sold space. The old stories are faint, and the new ones have yet to move in. I make a quick sketch of the apartment, pulling my tape from column line to column line and filling my sheet with dimensions. The red spot of my laser dances across the clear span of the roof trusses and lands on a white plaster surface. Somewhere below, a door closes, and the laser beam catches her shoulder as she comes up the stairs.

◆ ✢ ◆

Every client is not a lover. Not every client is a lover. But in some way, all clients are lovers.

◆ ✢ ◆

A friend tells me that the painter probably washed his brushes in jars of turpentine and brush cleaner. That he probably saved the dregs in a container, taking it to a facility periodically. I see the painter and his pail of runoff, both getting murkier over time.

◆ ✢ ◆

There was a period of time, after our last argument, when we did not speak. I moved away, and she did too. I was surprised when she sent me an email, saying that she had seen me through a window, passing by on the street. *What are you doing in town again?*

◆ ✢ ◆

In a flexible space, the millwork becomes key. Cabinets become closets become tables become shelves become screens. We start to talk about folding, turning, hiding, reciprocity. The language of everyday things gets loaded with meanings. We find ourselves face to face with our selves in a mirror when we close a door-wall, unable to look away.

◆ ⁑ ◆

She tells me that she will build out the interior herself. She lays out and frames the stud walls, toe nailing each vertical member to the bottom plate, heading out the doors and tying the assembly together with the top plate. The pencil in her hand marks a piece of spruce-pine-fir; the circular saw pauses, its foot resting on top of the lumber as she sights her mark. Her finger closes on the trigger, and the blade springs to life.

◆ ⁑ ◆

Before she became a carpenter, she used to work at a wine distributor's. They gave her bottles as gifts on occasion. I remember that a hundred bottles, give or take, would lie about her apartment, hidden behind furniture like cats. We would drink one and two more would watch us. They will need a home in the carriage house too.

◆ ⁑ ◆

The trades rough in as she works on the millwork at her shop. Lines of water, supply and waste, gas lines, junction boxes. Blue board hung and taped at the seams, and a skim coat of plaster. Hands unknown, even to me. I help to receive the plywood delivery at the shop, loading the sheets on a cart and moving them to the table saw. She lays each sheet down on the cross-cut sled, halving an eight-foot panel into two four-by-fours. Her hand grips the crank that raises the blade and turns. Teeth emerge from the throat of the saw. The language of the saw is an uncomfortable thing. The throat is a hole that does not really exist. Look in any manual. You will find the throat plate covering up the gap. You will find every last set screw described with a name and part number. But you will not find the void itself.

◆ ⊹ ◆

Superstudio and Archizoom are the collectives most people think of when they think of *critical Italian architecture from the 1960s*. That is, if they think of critical Italian architecture at all, or if they think of Italian architecture, or even just architecture. The work of Superstudio is a work of figures and grids. Bodies, naked and clothed, cities, dogs and cows, friends, families, one child or many, parties, protests—are enmeshed in grids of lines intersecting at right angles. The unit of the grid is practically scaleless, ranging from three centimetres to thirty metres, and the grid runs on to infinity. They proposed to turn off the flow of the American side of the Niagara Falls, temporarily, as the Army Corps of Engineers did in the summer of 1969, to build a rectangular basin with a mirrored, stainless steel finish. The flow would then be restored, and water would thunder back into the basin, filling it up in *33 minutes, no seconds and 94 hundredths*. During that time, water and reflected sky touch, throatless.

I live in a 49 square foot rectangle

Jisu Yang

She enters my space without asking, tickling my eyes, forcing me to step outside of the imagined reality. My eyes open up and my skin immediately senses the temperature of her breath. My sight gazes into her mouth. She consoles me by organizing a dance between the leaves and the wind. The actress comes in through her mouth to caress my dry skin.

I step outside, use my two fingers to grab her top and the bottom. I fold her into a 4x4 feet rectangle and gently placed her on top of stacked boxes. Then I lift the mattress up vertically to create a private studio. I sit on the stool of boxes. Placed my brushes on a raised coffee table to work on a painting that occupies half of the wall. Conforming to my weight, the boxes collapse. My body hits the ground and my feet knock over a paint bucket, spilling water all over the floor. Out of frustration, My palm lifts myself up against me. My vision goes hazy and I reappear in a flooded city.

Crowded street, people constantly crash into my shoulder. Flooded of people, I search for silence. Turning a corner into a compressed street, my two elbows are constantly in touch with the wall. The more I walk through, the more the crowd of the city is muted and the sound of relief appears. Reaching the end of the street, I find myself in the reflection of the ground. Tangled hair, collar dragged on my shoulder, unzipped bag.

Delicate strumming brought me back to reality. A soft melody floated in the air, coming from this man seated along the other side of the river. Tall and lanky with a five o' shadow, a white bunny seated at his left shoulder. An opened violin case. As he played, they all stopped to listen. A bridge connecting two worlds became a gateway for entering his melody. Melancholy, nostalgia, and welcoming. My fingers grabbed two coins from the back pocket and placed it on his case alongside with sparsely located coins.

This was one year ago.

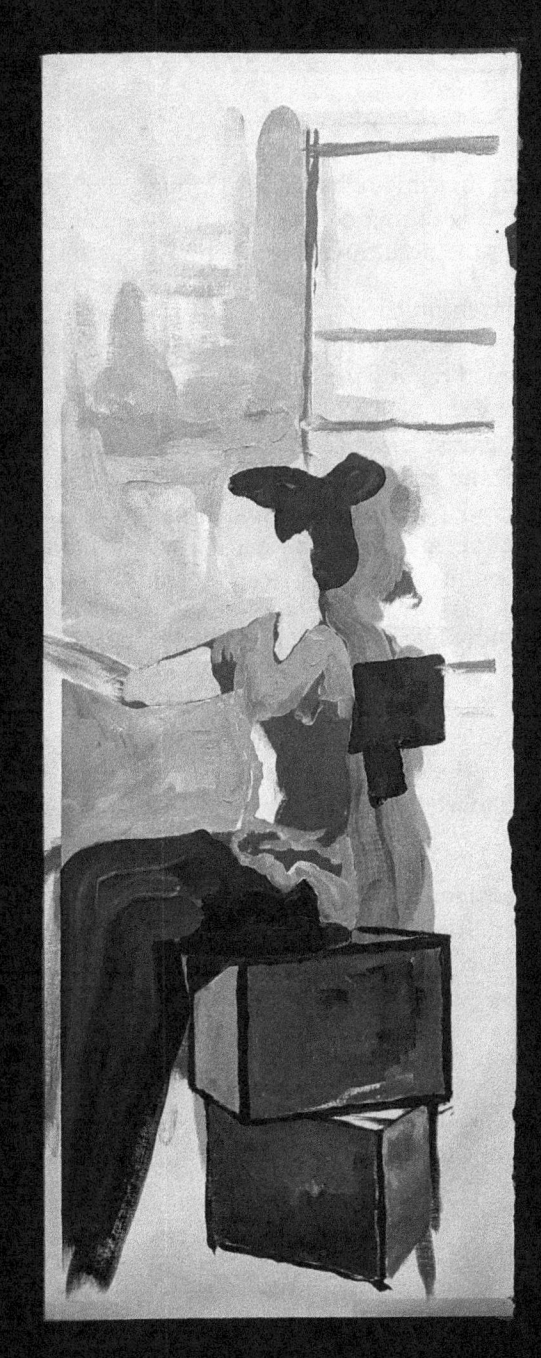

My Earth

Jisu Yang

The warm morning light pierces through cracks in the fog. Turning around, I step back inside, with my foot over the doorway, gently resting upon the earthen floor. Grains of sand accumulate between my toes and the dirt tracks my every footstep.

The room reminded me of an old earthen house, as the walls were deteriorating, barely supporting the low ceiling. Delicate cracks decorated the walls, and the room seemed to only inhabit one old master. As I stood, the light began to lightly dance along the debris of the floor, stopping upon an array of tall earthen pots lined up against the wall. Each pot was labeled with large strips of beige tape; hay, clay, sand, and soil. The only other object present was an old dusty wooden table, with mason jars lined up, encrusted with dried clay. My eyes look for a place for me to explore, to inhabit the space without intruding. The hinges of the wooden door behind me creaks, to a deep but gentle voice.

The Japanese master brings a bucket of hay balls; posidonia which are rolled hays from the beach of Sardegna. He grabs a piece of posidonia, requests attention from the crowd, and starts using his fingertips to peel tiny pieces of hay. I grab a ball of hay and feel the texture of the beach with my finger tips. The more I peel, the more I smell and sense the presence of salt in the ball.

A quarter of water, one fifth of soil, two fifths of sand, and two fifths of posidonia. I dumped my two hands into the bucket. She is confused. All her bodies are scattered. My fingers untangled her hair. Unclogged her nose. As I push and pull, my muscle feels her resistance. Her hair starts wrapping around her nose. Her body starts to become one as things are more unified. My sweat crawls down the skin into her body.

The master unrolls a giant leather bundle. He grabs one of the plates, scoops her up and pastes her on the surface. His entire body moves. He rubs her against the surface. From left to right, smearing across the surface of the plate, with just enough pressure to flatten her body. The sharp plate slices her texture creating stratified landscape.

My hand grabs the tool and perceives the softness of the wood handle. My wrist feels the weight of her body. My line of sight engages with the water that connects my view with her view. My body is moving constantly while my bicep forces the rest of the muscle to maintain tranquility. She is consoled.

Every moment of pulse is reflected by her pulses on the skin.

My earth is created.

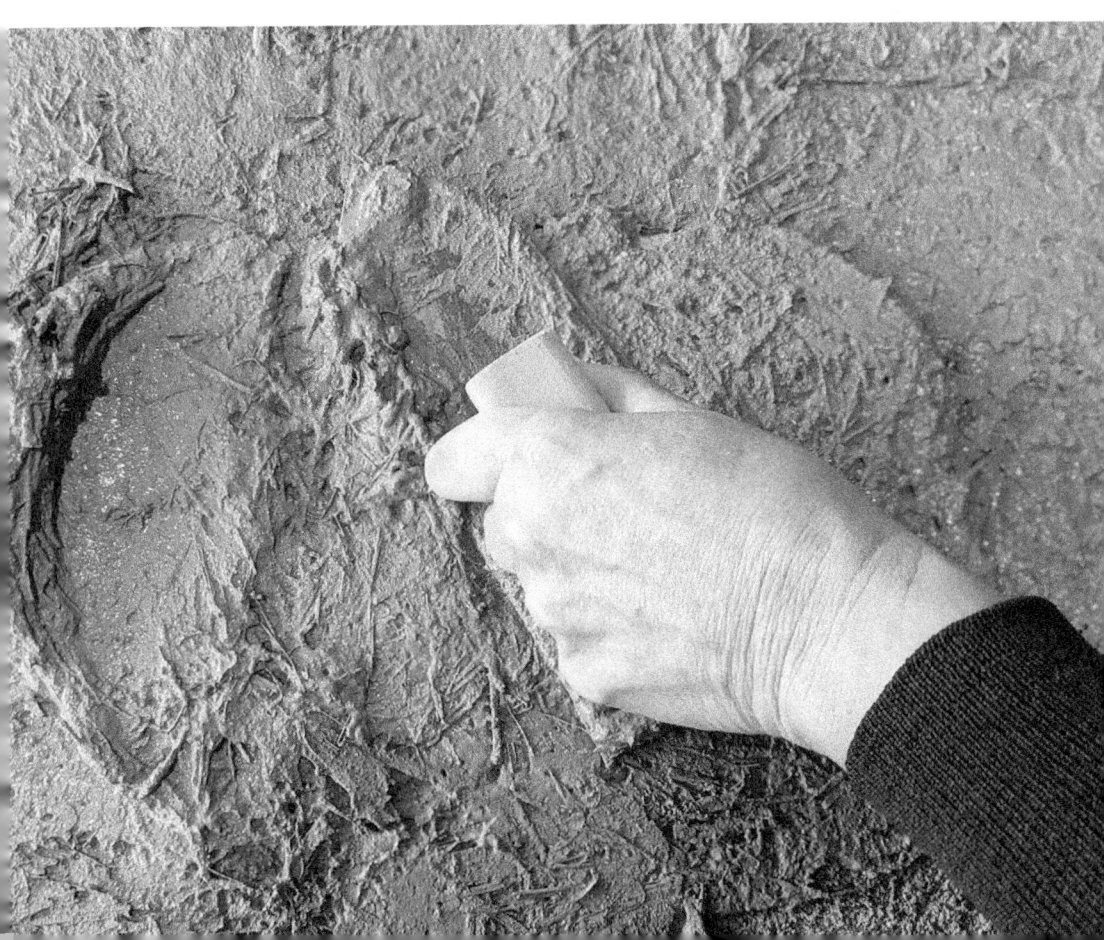

Central Park Walk

Alice Momm

Walking in Central Park –
A quotidian affair
A heated slog to work
A slow and rambling return

I am seeking space
Away from people and machines
motors, drills, horns, shouts, air-conditioned hum

I am searching for signs
of other kinds of being
some quiet magic
a cool blanket portal
some liminal calm

So I focus my lens away from what displeases
    discarded masks
        crunched-up water bottles
           torn condom pack
                sparrows with Cheetos
                    floating plastic bags

To quiet dramas everywhere

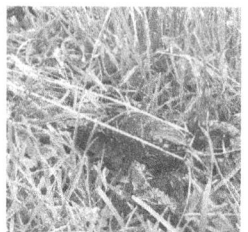

Crayfish muscling through the grass

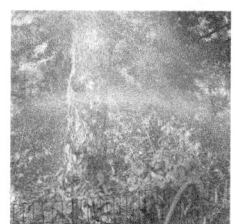

Rainbow birthed from a sprinker

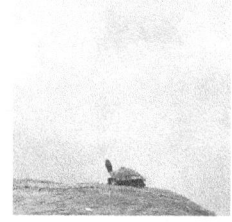

Turtle in the vast beyond

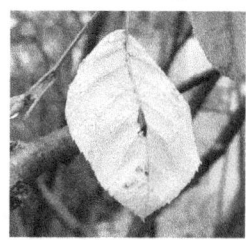

A little velvet tear

Shadowed flight across the sky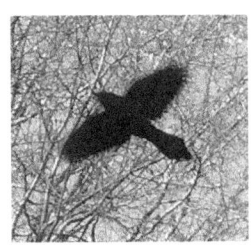

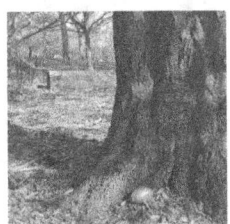
A golden egg

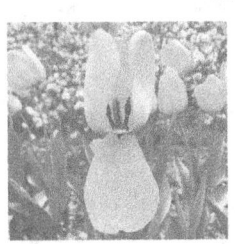
A peek inside

and once
a green balloon
that floated down into my waiting hand.

Leaves alight green bright still but not for long and

baring of the finite body against the infinite, both spiritual and earthly

denaturing

(2)

Ants, Strange and Particular

Becky Vartabedian

EXERCISE

Find a word.

Say it over and over and over until it sounds weird.

Catch (if you can) that moment at which the word turns weird.

What is that like? What happens? How long does it take for that word to return to normal? What do you feel when the word returns to its place?

Andrew shared work with us that developed around autoantonyms (or contranyms).[1] These are words that share spelling but offer contradictory meanings; the example on Wikipedia is cleave, which can mean both to cut and to bind, depending on the context. Andrew's work also included words that are similar except for one letter (i.e., *closed, close*) that accomplish the same kind of effect, managing to stall thought on its uninterrupted path of capturing and making sense of words together. The poem was short and deeply affecting in that it caused all of us to stop, to roll the phrases over a bit more before moving on.

This led us to a discussion of the role defamiliariziation plays in the work of writing. We can understand this straightforwardly as the exercise I suggest above, trying to catch (if we can) that moment at which the familiar turns weird. The idea is that there's something to that moment, to the weird pause before the word goes back to normal, back to its place. I have been thinking a fair bit about defamiliarization in my theoretical work, considering the "grammar of things" in and around me. This started as some inquiry about iron salts in cyanotype photographs but extends pretty quickly to my yard.

There are two substantial ant hills on our lot: one is on the front easement and the other is on the back part of our backyard. They are roughly parallel to one another. I have a friendly relationship with these ants and their places; I speak to them, greet them in the morning, and out of courtesy tell them when I'm coming nearby with the lawn mower, being sure to always mow around them. This pro-ant disposition comes from my reading of work by Deborah Gordon and particularly

---

1   *cf.* Andrew Helton, "Petalless/Petalous," page 181

her essay about the memory of an ant colony. In that first reading, pests became residents, and residents that potentially have a longer memory than the twelve years I've lived in my house. The yards are not only mine if I can make any claim to their being mine at all.

It's weird.

On Thursday night my sister and I were talking about particular experiences and inquiring about the capacity for these kinds of experiences to teach us something. Ironically, we were not talking about *a* particular experience, but were discussing the value of these in general. Anyway, we agreed that there is a real richness to the particular, to the precise and singular things that present themselves to us for our engagement. We also agreed that there's a tendency to rush and categorize these, to give the particular experience some kind of universal meaning; in doing so we tend to miss what's true in the presentation *itself*, in the phenomenon unfolding before our eyes. In my line of work, this tendency toward categorization is a tendency toward the stability offered by ideas of true and false, ideas that allow us–with some speed, which is sometimes necessary–to make decisions and prescribe courses of action in relation to the thing unfolding before us. I'm not saying this is bad, but I wonder if we couldn't do with a little more *weird*, a little more *strange*, a willingness to resist–for just a little bit longer–that move back toward the familiar.

The thing about the ants is still weird. My questions about "ownership" and "mineness" and all of that are unresolved because those ants are about their business whether I like it or not. I could bomb them out of the backyard, but something about the encounter took that option off the table for me. The ants, in their everyday way of being (including their carrying forward the memory of their colony), called into question what I thought was settled; the ants demanded my attention in a way I couldn't offer before because I assumed they had nothing for me. My assumptions weren't necessarily wrong, but they were incomplete.

There's no secret message here; I'm really stumped by the ants in the backyard, to the further perplexity of my husband and, most certainly, the two dogs who have had unfortunate encounters with these ants, either by eating one that squirmed all the way down (the apprentice) or having one chomp its paw (the teacher). However,

I think we can learn something in this about how we are living now, especially in this particular moment of unrest, this particular moment on the cusp of some things that should be 'normal' that are decidedly not (back to school, elections, democracy), this particular moment when we are looking around to make sense of what is happening. Perhaps what we need - for just a little while - is to allow this strange to unfold, to see who and what are inviting us to cooperate and to share space, to put the brakes on that moment toward resolution and see the things we thought settled get cracked open and cracked up.

See what comes next, see what comes new.

Self Reliance

Nicole Le

When the coyote howls and she is not answered, it is the silent starting gun for a cascade of internal mechanisms, locks and gears churning in and out of place as her body transforms to produce two, three times as many pups, like a prophet multiplying loaves. In the absence of her community, she takes it upon herself to rectify their extinction. Americans laced the earth with poison, baited the coyote relentlessly, culled its population some years by 70%, only to see the pack numbers resurge year after year undeterred. The packs howl and yip every night in census, counting their numbers, then retreat to their dens and let the natural magic stir inside them.

Some birds seem to matter more as metaphor

Alice Momm

SWAN

me
just old enough
to peer out the back window
of a speeding station wagon
on the Long Island Expressway
split-second sighting
a swan's eye
met mine.

she
half plastered to the road
long neck and
one wing reaching to the sky
straining for flight
as cars raced by.

CROW

My friends watched Hitchcock's "Birds"
but I declined
content with my own colloquies
cawing with crows
bounding through trees

SPARROW

Sparrows
in dirt baths
know just how to shake it
whipped up whishy whizzing wings
beaks dip down to spoon and fling
out out little mites!
still
you might hardly notice
the chip chip chipping
from their tiny pools of earth

PASSENGER PIGEON

Martha
last of her kind
who lived and died in the Cincinnati Zoo
was met in my periphery
enshrined in a glass vitrine
She led me on a journey
unearthing avian histories
and taught me to love
the strutting puffed up
mating dance of pigeons
on my street

Blessing

Nicole Le

I don't realize my back is burnt until a drop of sweat plummets down the side of my ribcage, and my skin burns in the wake of its tiny tail. I turn over and put my shirt over my face. The sun beats through a cloudless sky and the concrete warms. Big reds and oranges bloom behind my eyelids. The dogs nose around in the trench behind me. It is summer and there are rats, mice, lizards in from the abutting canyon. Claws scuttle rocks, rummage among buckets, tarpaulin, fishing poles, yard stuff. I am sleepy with sun.

The heels of my hands press the reds and oranges into bruising blossom blues, like night, like night of street lamps, like nights when I sneak away and throw myself into the company of strangers and their full joy body recklessness. Like Alizah, who invited me into the living room of plants heavy with never-ending Eden nakedness until four in the blue morning, who came outside in bare feet to stand with me. We waited for the taxi, and I knelt and put my hands on the tops of her feet to warm them until the clunking purr of the car came around the corner. The driver asked in a velvet accent, "Why did you do that?"

"It's so cold out."

He kept his eyes ahead. "That is a blessing where I come from," he said. Alizah is forever consecrated.

A bark jolts me back into this heat. It continues, insisting. I peel myself off the ground and walk to the trench, look down. The dog barks manically at an enormous snake curled round itself.

My brother comes when he hears my yell. We lock the dogs away, and I send him down into the trench, urge him to be careful, but it doesn't matter because the snake is caught, unable to move in a mess of fishing net propped against the wall of the trench.

We crouch closer, linger longer to see where it is caught. Its body is partially suspended, like a fucked-up hammock floating an inch above the dirt. The snake twists away, then tries to lunge at us, but tangles again and traps itself further. Our curiosity edges into the helpless, into the urgent. I put on a gardening glove, use various knives, try to separate the netting to better see where the snake is caught. My brother waves his own knife and yells.

We find the source. A thread of net has caught under one of its tightly layered scales, and in the snake's writhing, the origin point has slipped deeper. The snake pulls one way, the net holds fast, and the snake is skinning itself before our eyes. The harder it pulls, the more muscle is exposed. The primordial diamond head encased in perfect, God-born snakeskin erupts into six-inch swath of flesh. We gag on the plummet into grotesque, and the heat of our panic spills out. Our fear of death pours out in frothy hatefulness, as if we ourselves had taken the snake and yanked its scales off in our bare hands. We hate each other more than we ever have as we terrify ourselves into action, work desperately with our useless fingers. The snake twists again and again, freaking itself open while we watch.

We are in tears, mad at the snake, mad at the coastal desert for its careening valleys and falcons and irrepressible hordes of rabbits and suburbia and the packing in of lizards and sparrows and coyotes and people and dogs and snakes, mad at this death in our trench, mad at our weakness, our realization that we are so afraid. It is easier to shake our knives at one another. Shut up you fucking you fuck what the fuck what are you doing you're doing it wrong goddamn god what did you do? There is no tree cover. We stand under the sun, overburdened with useless equipment and clothing, and it burns our outsides and melts us to sweat. The snake wanted to pass through unbidden, but we caught it with our mess and our failings, with our uncontrollable usness.

I force my hand to steady and cut the netting away, lifting parts of the snake's limpening body with my other hand. At this, my brother quiets.

I free the snake; it slinks with half-heart into a pail. My brother picks up the handle and turns away. My hands shake hard. I didn't mean what I said. I watch as he climbs the slope of the yard and enters the canyon, red bucket swinging gently like giant fruit in his hand. His figure shrinks and ripples. I cannot tell how far he will go to free the snake.

Oweynagat

Dana Brinson

Oweynagat
Mouth
open
under a lane
swallows me whole
Slide down tongue left
there to ease y/our way into
The belly. The womb. The tomb.
Climb to the clit Hands in
prayer Silence makes
room for the
heartbeat
.drip.
consecrated
chalice We claim
you   Tlachtga   whispers
Light enough that you won't stay
Dark enough that you won't stay
away. stalactite-to-be-or-tears .drip.
my heart found her song
CrowRavenOwlSwan
witnessed in the pressing
Dark Sisters of the
heart
.drip.
anointed
times three
out the way in–pushed
forth to the sun
undone and
Done

Broken Oak

Dana Brinson

Oak broken open oh god
Three centuries gone
Leaves alight green bright still but not for long and
Not forever as your
Branches bare against the endless azure
Promised each day from Yule to Ostara and
Recommitted through Samhain in emerald-gold boa whispering
Roots grasping at the air for breath great wind left you gasping
As I wretched at the turn whipped off and ran
To you crying twisting and falling with you
Devastation through

A Brief Memoir of Childhood Refracted through a Love of Plants

Leslie Berns

Held between four year old fingertips up close to brown, bright eyes, a star-shaped flower the size of a dime. Pointed petals and berries the color of green peas. The minute violet and canary yellow details of its visage pressed forever into my memory. A weed at the back of our backyard where my first friend Kathy McGloin and I played. Our running games included make-believe stories of princesses and princes instantly dying upon eating the poisonous berries.

Was there a path along a row of tall columnar trees at the back of the backyard where the flowers and berries grew within our reach?

Once the pandemic has passed, I'll make the seven-hour drive to the back of the backyard of the house at 316 Athens Boulevard, in the Town of Tonawanda, in Buffalo, New York. And scout whether a row of tall columnar trees with a path is still there, or once might have been.

It feels odd and sad to be curious about revisiting a distant backyard.

Maybe I can identify the weed–now dignified as a native plant, its resiliency better understood–by searching flora of western New York online. It's not possible anyway now to travel to New York from Maryland, without quarantining. Nor is it possible to return to a plant in a place drastically altered by time.

Although in 1964 we *did* return to plants in a place, and people. We flew from Buffalo to Miami to Kingston, Jamaica. Then drove to the country in a Volkswagen with Petula Clark on the radio belting out her hit song *Downtown*. When we got to Top Hill we got out of the car and walked the rest of the way down a rocky, red-dirt path to reach the homestead where my great-great grandparents are buried.

My mother and we met aunts and uncles and cousins for the first time. My great aunt Rosa's outdoor kitchen, mango and coconut palm trees, bird of paradise flowers, and tall grasses surrounding above-ground graves, a continuous cycle of being born, growing and eating food, living and dying.

That same year, a couple of months after being back home in Buffalo we moved six miles away.

I can corroborate the year by vividly recalling where I was and what I was doing when President Kennedy was assassinated in 1963, November 22nd. I still lived in the house with the star-shaped flowers.

Upstairs in the room with a telephone, my parents' bedroom, my mother was crying–wailing–on the phone with her friend Shirley Massik. Her face contorted. Yanking the hem of her shirt with my right hand, in my left hand a ketchup and bologna sandwich that I was *not* enjoying. I was trying to get my mother's attention to tell her *I want to go back to mustard.*

So it must have been the summer of '64 that we moved into a newly built house at 270 Robin Hill Drive in Williamsville in time for my sister to start third grade and for me to begin kindergarten. Several tall, mature oak and maple trees stood spaced apart in a more ample, unfenced yard than the narrow, fenced yard of the first house.

Each fall of the seven my family spent on Robin Hill, when the canopy let go of its foliage the yard became a pool filled with textured, wave-edged, paper leaves. My friend Carla Baver and I tirelessly raked the leaves into a monumental pile as high as we could build it. We took turns running towards the colorful mound of confetti, diving into it and landing buried beneath its cool, grainy, earthy cologne.

Again! Again! Again!

After playing in the leaves for hours, when Carla, or perhaps Beth had gone home for dinner and after I had eaten my meal, I went back outside and repeated the ritual by myself with just as much glee until it got dark and it was time to go indoors.

As we grew further away from childhood my friends and I played less and less often in the leaves. The last time Beth and I did, she, a year older, stepped back from it sooner than I. From the sidelines she watched as I pretend-played for a few too many minutes. A somewhat decent performance–she may have even believed it. But like Beth, I knew in my bones that the joy of playing with such pure abandon could not be recovered. Our bodies were too big to run and leap exactly as they had, and our minds had moved elsewhere, too.

The following summer, in 1971, we moved from Buffalo to Newport Beach, California. We drove off, from friends and family, and Buffalo's winters, in a used 1967 gold Cadillac my father bought to match the moving picture of his golden dream.

A week later we arrived at night at our *Harbor View Home* at 1939 Port Edward Place. We peered through the ground floor windows and pictured ourselves occupying the house's empty interior. Reflected in the glass, a southern California landscape of palm trees, succulents, and bird-of-paradise flowers.

On Pacific Coast Highway, at the southern edge of Corona del Mar, north of Laguna Beach, we stayed at the Kirkwood Motel until the moving van arrived with our belongings. The two-story, U-shaped motel embraced a built-in illuminated pool. Every night for a week I dove under the water and swam and splashed around with a girl my age, my first friend in California. We quickly bonded as 'new best friends' but she was just passing through on holiday.

It turned out, so was I. My mother and I returned east after a year followed by my father and sister several months later. Our California sojourn unfolded in 1971 and folded in 1972. A disruptive year, for sure, infused with the potent, gorgeous aroma of jasmine flowers, a fragrance from a dream.

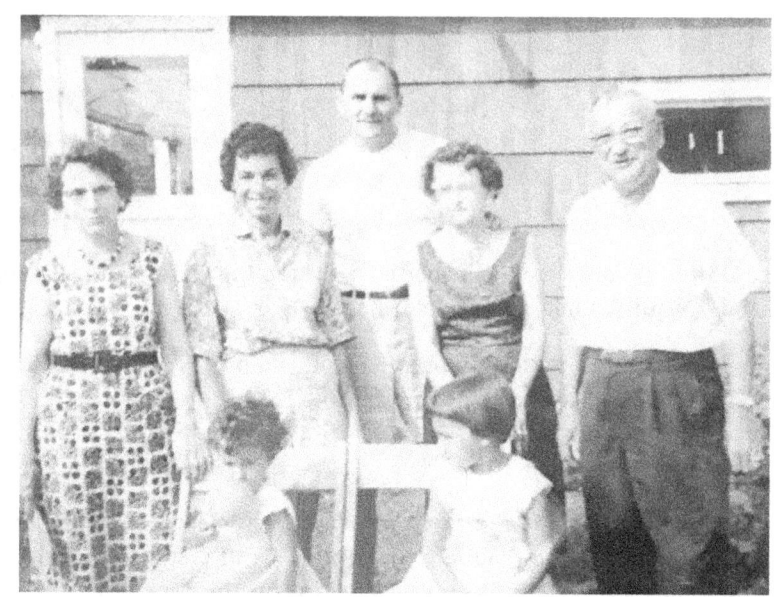

Town of Tonawanda, NY

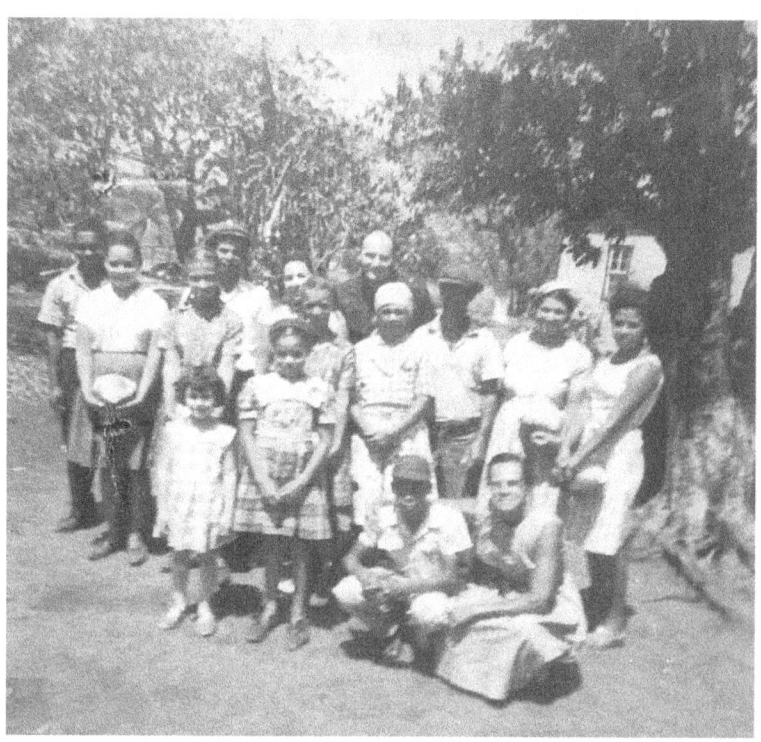

Top Hill, Jamaica

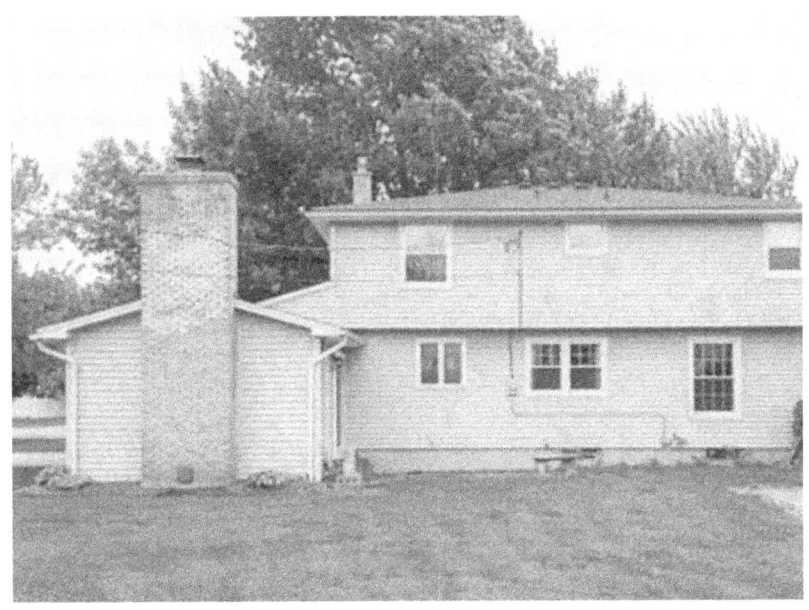

Williamsville, NY

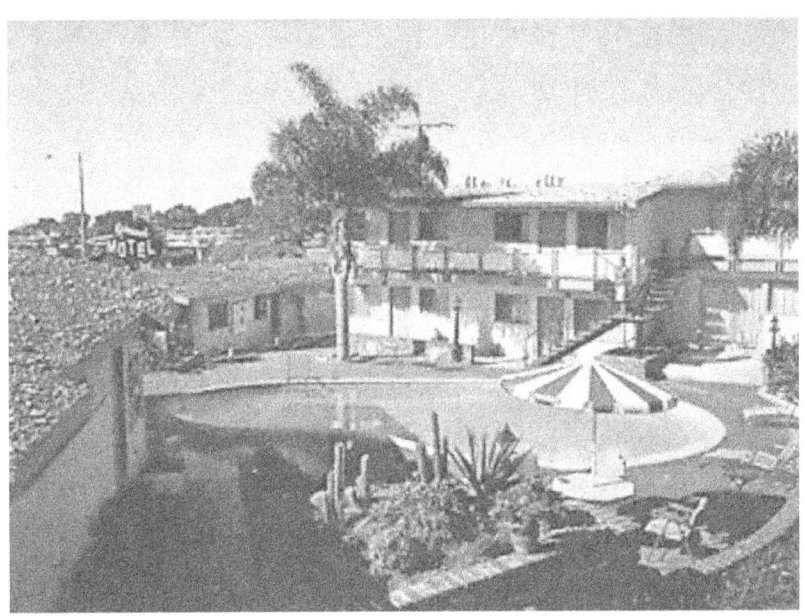

Corona del Mar, CA

Release

Leslie Berns

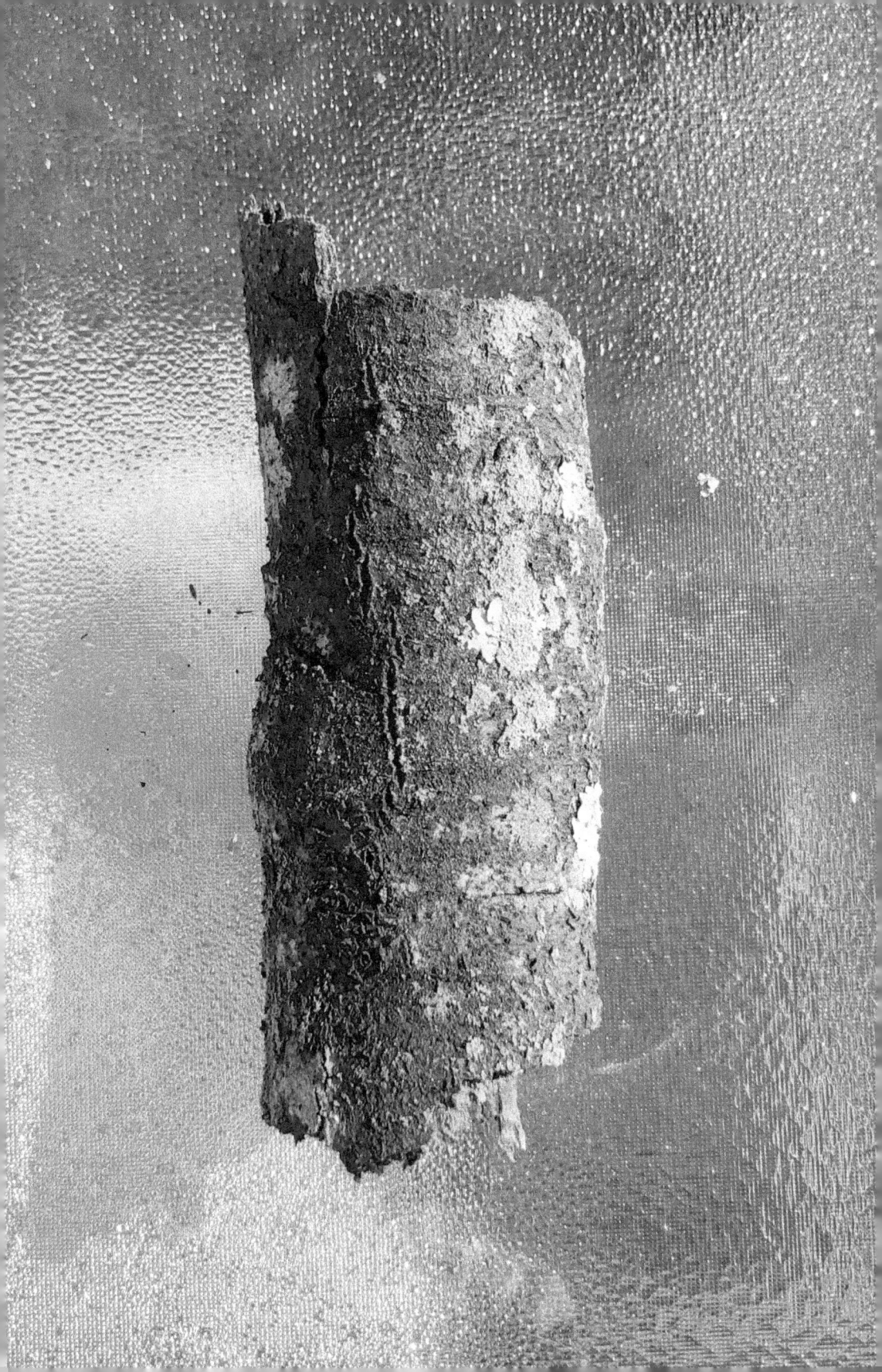

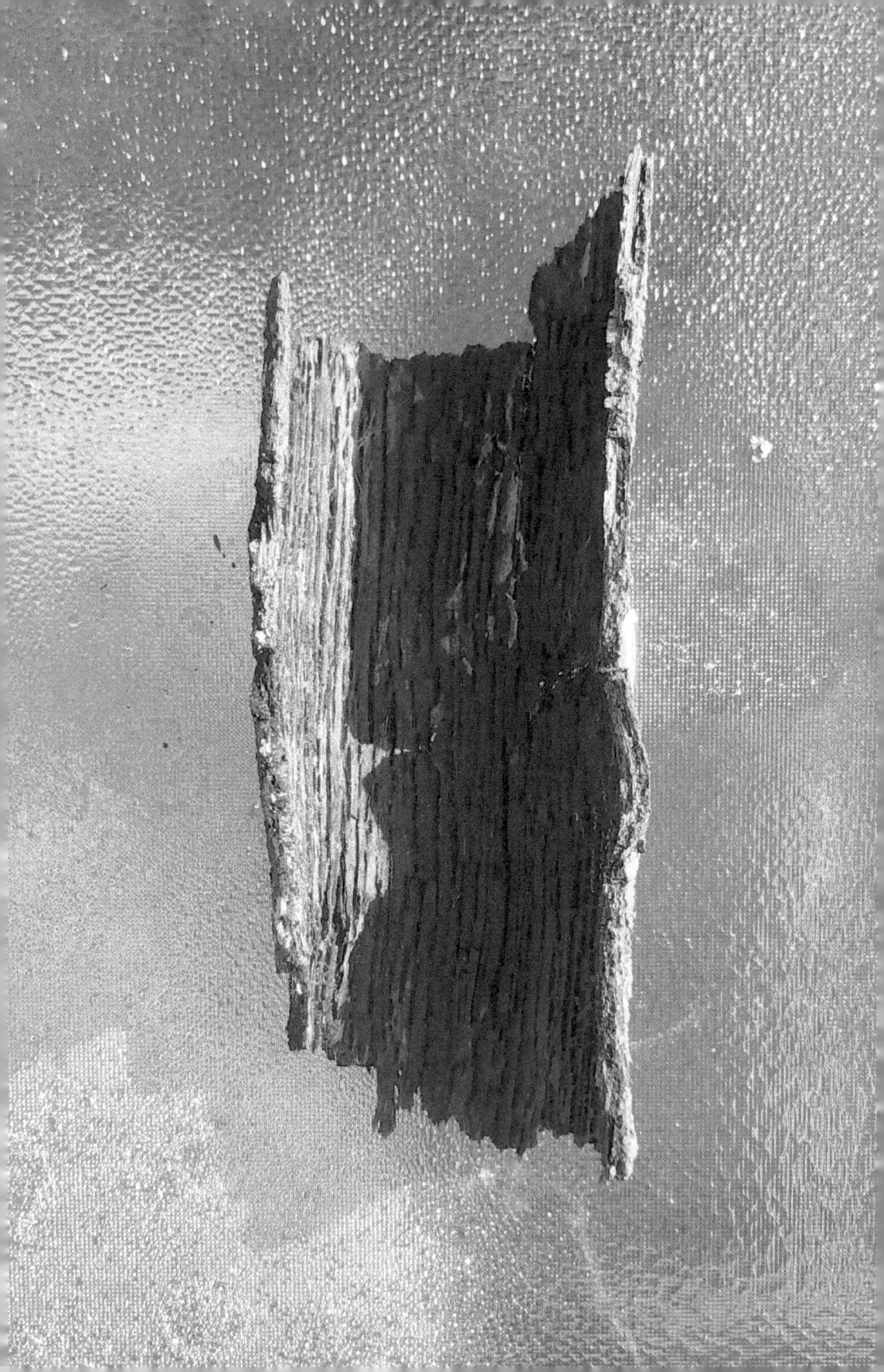

Morning wood, wood morning.
Wood morning, morning wood!
Wood. Morning.

It's Good to Know the Cows You're Milking

Annie Jacobs

I feel a tinge of anticipation when a milking session begins. Each one is something of an event, even when nothing out of the ordinary happens. After first cleaning up after them and giving them their grain and sweet-smelling hay, the hour or so I spend milking these six Jersey cows has an intensity to it. Partly, they're just so big. Last year I was milking goats, where the scale of everything is comparatively tiny. If a goat was acting out her capricious tendencies, and refused to leave the milking parlor through the exit door after our ten minutes together, I could use all of my body weight to get her moving. The cows weigh approximately a ton, give or take, and that's not a size that I have any hope of competing with.

Fortunately, the cows don't seem to know their own power. The occasional startled looks on their faces, and their quickness to spook at a sudden noise or a bucket out of place, remind me of the animals of my teenage years - the horse. They are flight animals.

I have been shy my entire life, and I struggle with insomnia and anxiety, panic, and bouts of depression. I don't want to whine about my mood issues. But I do want to note how the energy of these cows can have a nervous edge to it, that I relate to that, and that, when we're together, I feel all of it ease. I feel good as soon as I'm walking them in from pasture, and I can be sure that any kind of angst I came to the farm with will have diffused, or transmuted, within a short time. As for the six cream-colored beauties, they too seem comforted by being in the milking parlor. I know it's largely the release of their udders (and oxytocin), which have been filling up since the last milking. But they are as clocked in as any of us, and are well aware of who gets milked when in the lineup, so that Abbey has already begun turning around in her stall before I've started walking toward her.

When tall, moody Glisten is in the parlor and I'm preparing her for milking by cleaning her udders and disinfecting her teats, she might or might not be in a feisty spell, and I have to be careful of where I position myself lest I get a kick. But once the milk machine is on, she takes a tremendous breath in -- which fills her mid section and lifts it up, like a dancer or a yogi -- and then she breaths out, and an immense peace settles on everything. The milk is flowing through four inflations (one on each teat) and pumped through a hose into the milk can. I am squatting and my chest is open in a position that feels remarkably similar to the yogic squat, or Garland pose. These ten minutes or so with Glisten are a highlight, even if a little tense. Glisten marks the climax of milking for me, or at least a turn of events, where the conflict continues for the next three complicated cows. It's important to know the cows you're milking in order to get it right. I can't imagine what it's like for farmers who milk 30, or 300, cows.

I was vegetarian for a very long time and also vegan. These days the whole milk yogurt I make from the milk that comes from Abbey, Glisten, and their cohorts, and other animal products from the farm, make up a significant part of my diet. But because I know what it takes –how much presence is required, how much patience–I've begun again to question even the most humanely-sourced products I can find at a store. The ratio of person to cows (1:6) feels just about right to give quality attention. I'm not sure what I'll eat when I leave this farm.

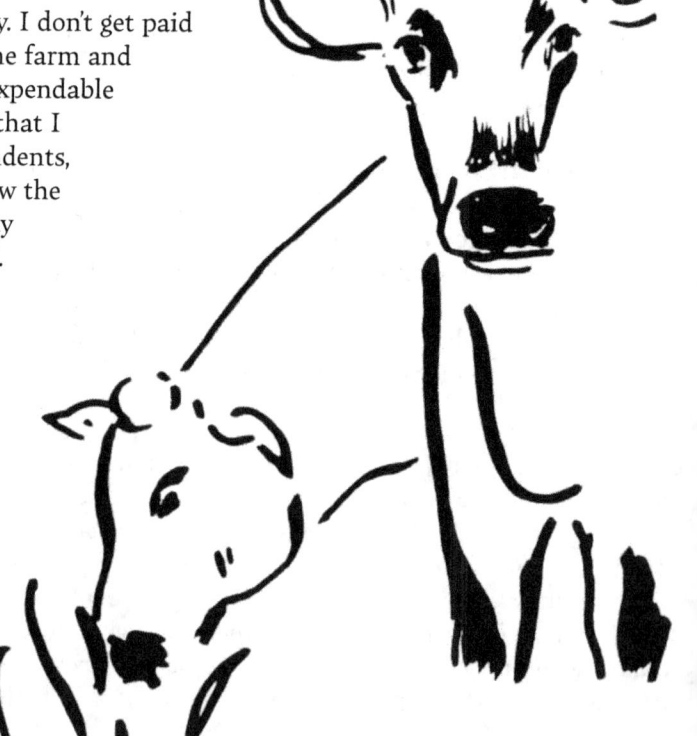

So, I am extremely lucky. I don't get paid much for my work on the farm and I really don't have any expendable income. I am fortunate that I don't have debt or dependents, and I'm able to live below the poverty line and still stay warm and eat quite well. I get plenty of sunshine and exercise, and com-ments on my bulging arm muscles. Writers and artists, as we know, have to have more than one job. Some pay, some don't; all of them at least offer some kind of fuel–be it inspiration, regular-ity, or a way to get out of our heads and onto our feet a little.

My cow job feeds me on a number of planes. So, I am extremely lucky. At least this year.

The cows have been out on spring grass since last week, and as a result, after my alarm goes off at 5 am and I'm relishing a few minutes with tea and breakfast, and low light, and a little birdsong, I find myself speaking these lines in my head. What are these lines, oh yes, I realize, I'm reciting one of my favorite poems, and for no reason other than that my daily reality has conjured it from memory. The poem is Robert Frost's "Birches."

" . . . as he went out and in to fetch the cows . . ." There is something unspeakably good about doing that, and I wonder if it's in our DNA, as coevolution- ary theory would suggest. Indeed, we and dairy animals have lived and worked together for a very long time. I don't know how long I'll be living this dream, which might be romantic, but is certainly not at all easy; I am savoring it: the give and take of farming, the magic of grass turning to milk, and, more than any- thing else by far, the opportunity to know, and be known by, this one small herd. One could do worse.

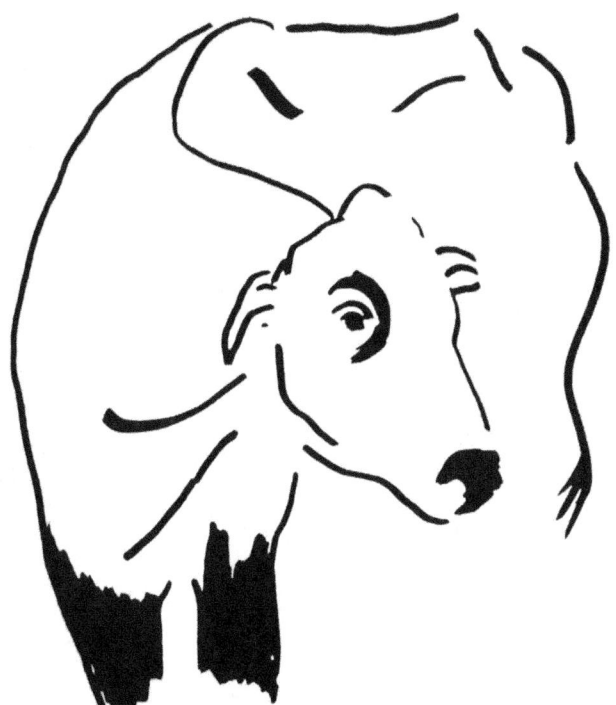

Sight-sited

Alice Momm

1   (oversight)

Outside the American market in La Paz, Bolivia,
I held my mother's hand.

Outside the market by the dry riverbed
a young boy led an old woman in a bowler hat.

A certain slant of light cut across the woman's face
illuminating skin
stretched taught above her sunken cheeks
where not even
the ghosts of eyes
remained

Palms beseeching for
mercy
some change

My mother kept on walking toward the market door
though I strained to see the why
She looked too long at the sun, said mom.

Even at five I knew
that some boys went barefoot and I
to the beauty parlor for a pixie cut.
that for some
a ray of sun
was the maddest dream
never mind the hubris of Icarus
whose feathered flight
beyond the fire-strewn Andes
still soared through thinning atmosphere
before drowning in the sea

Outside the American Market
grief took hold as metaphor
the wolf lay down in grandma's bed
And some change
was never change enough.

2   (out of sight)

My mother lost her mother when she was just sixteen
        after
two years on Welfare Island
        after
bed sores and despair
        after
a paralyzing stroke
My mother was a saint, is all she's ever told me.

but once she added this...
My mother never asked for anything and she didn't get it either.
and after her mother's funeral, they found, hidden in a basement trunk,
the complete works of Balzac.

3   (sight)

Do you remember?
Little Forest?
And the birthday party just for me?
We played in a shady clearing
under turned-over rocks
pill bugs, millipedes and milky white larvae
decomposing leaves
smells of loamy earth

Then one long strand of colored yarn
placed in each grubby little hand.
Follow this–mom said.
Hooray for adventures!
Criss-crossing around friends
over scarlet oaks and fallen logs
to the pot of gold at the yarn trail's end
skillfully disguised as a pumpkin.

4   (insight)

 Lately mom's been feeling terrific
She tells me this as we try to unpack her renewed vigor
just weeks ago
in group chats we sisters spoke unsettling words
covert Covid conversions

But something changed and now
mom is effervescent with late-born revelations
wisdom learned from daughters
such fascinating articles in the New York Times
the joys of youtube yoga
tidal waves of mindfulness spill forth unabated
the wonder of it all!

She reaches out her slender arm
for me to support her crooked frame
as we walk toward the park bench
to get a little sun
watch the goings on

Oh, look at all the sparrows hopping! says mom.

Hmmmmmmm...

Alice Momm

At the round wooden table on the screened-in porch
sunlight filtering through the green below
in the percolating buzz of late-morning ease
what spills forth unbidden
from coffee-wet lips
for no one to hear

    Oh my god, I am in love with peace

The soft-rustling-leaves-in-the-wind kind of peace
The trills and chirps of sing-song birds
avian symphony quaking bush
kind of peace

Oh balmy breeze
that rolls softly up my back until it spills over shoulders
to dance with the ferns beyond.

I am in love with water
    Not the distant sea but this little lake
borrowed for the weekend
too soon let go

And to the muted calm
of underwater
full immersion lover me
velvet skin yielding
to bubbles that rise along thighs
rays of sunlight piercing
through the yellow-green murk

of living things
little stings from minnow kisses
the tumbling/soaring/coupling of dragonflies
that swoop above and sometimes land
on a floating leaf

one wingbeat
an occasional hawk

I am in love with the peace of this piece of land
the unheard missives of trees
cicada buzz and fireflies
wet moss underfoot
squishy magic carpet
caressing happy toes
hoppy toads
and knowing when
to let it grow

Hmmmmmmmmmmmmmmmmmmmmm

"am I enough of this" to be 'authentic.'

the grounding in the particular that brings us in closer

object lessons

(3)

Moving Like Water

Becky Vartabedian

Last night we were sitting on the deck and I apologized for moving the boxes, which I moved with unthinking urgency, clumsily and lacking orderliness. I shoved them in the bin and would have kept doing it had you not stopped me. I was possessed with the spirit of my patriline, a spirit that responds to solicitations from the world with smash, bang, jam, shove, and almost-but-not-quite-right. Garbage disposals and indoor plumbing, half-built homes, keys that don't fully fit their lock (but do so just enough so you don't bother to change them).

Anyway, it was just after I apologized about the boxes and my possession by the ghosts of crash-and-smash and just-enough that you told me how, while you were away for the week you were working on moving like a bag of water, transforming self-understanding from roped muscle, flesh and bone and sinew to something that cannot move without all its bulk tipping to one side. This, you said, is really impossible to describe but when you are telling me your face breaks into a wide grin and your eyes light in a way I only see once or twice a year. Rare jewels.

You took hold of my arm, one hand cradling my bicep and the other under my forearm. Still grinning, you asked me to give you the weight of my arm and all of the sudden I didn't know how to do that; I thought I was doing it but I could feel the ways I was still holding myself, arm linked in socket to stiffened shoulder, something deep in the limb resists.

You let go, laid on the deck, said to me that moving like water is a bubbling up and then you did it, you moved that way and I was astonished and ashamed.

This morning my fingernails are dirty from moving the boxes.

Bone Readings

Nicole Le

You cannot read a radiograph in the light, so they sit in the dark, lights strapped to foreheads, covering their third eyes, searching for the abnormalities illuminated like underwater ghosts shimmering out of a shipwreck.

Her throwing arm is useless, she said. She takes pills to sleep, then dreams she walks through the house holding a severed arm on fire

Aha! There it is (a ghost wriggles out of the dark): her bones crash into one another where they should embrace softly like lovers. Like lovers in mid-air who press their cheeks and breast and belly against the tiny sliver of space that sleeps between them, bending into hollows to hold each other up in a feat against gravity.

I see the problem, one might say.

Let us roll onto our opposite side and look quietly upon the other pair: the quiet pair, the painless pair, the lover bones with strength to spare.

Be soothed by their celestial spooning

Take solace in a perfect tuning

Revel in the bones that sing,

Couple private, commune unseen.

But a strange thing: these bones, too, fight tooth and nail. They clash into each other as if they wished to trade places, crumbled faces mangling kiss after kiss.

What begets the flaming limb, then? What to do if cupping bodies are not solace from pain?

They sit in the dark covering their third eyes, searching with squinted eyes for light.

Object Love 1

Nicole Le

With my whole body I do thee worship. Lighter, my lover: the little one, the big one. The lemon meringue one. The brown one in the car. The one in my cabinet, pink like girlish sparkle chapstick. Sometimes I leave you in the rain, guiltily. And still when I sit with you on the porch in the sun, you come to life with a few clicks—object love. I can't get myself to turn on. I shake and shake, and nothing will catch. You are so consistent; I am filled with hope that you will light. You're a wonder; I hope for the possible. Orpheus and Eurydice did the same, walked in the dark, hoping. If that boy of longing had you, would he have doubted so much?

I throw you everywhere. Is this the feeling of total domination? I can hold you in my pocket, in my purse, between my teeth. Lover, let me bite you hard, harder than I've ever bit. But you will end up cracking my teeth. I won't win, will never win, as hard as I try to destroy you. I know you will light when I say so, you yielding thing. Yield to me. I love you. God, I love you, please don't leave me. I will let someone borrow you, but jealously.

Object Love 2

Nicole Le

On Friday, I pout my lips, pitch my voice accordingly, and fish for someone to reach out to me at the art show. I loiter at the taxidermist's table, fingering a rabbit's foot. She flirts me into buying a $10 silver ring instead; I slip it onto my left ring finger where it's a perfect fit.

All day, I admire it. I remember the last time I had a ring which sat perfectly on that finger, an enormous gold gauntlet I played with incessantly through college. I look at this tiny silver band and think to myself how it doesn't really signify anything, but if it did, it would be a symbol of some life and time together.

I like the way it looks too much. I've never been so taken with my own hands. The fingers look so slender, finally aristocratic for the first time in a life rife with nail biting. I don't play with this ring; it is a perfect ergonomic addition to my ensemble. I hold my perfect hand out in front of me and wonder if I'm a liar.

On Sunday, I am more anxious. I've been out in the cold all day and my hands throb. I get a massage at a parlor in Chinatown. The old lady massages my hands and asks about my husband. I am a liar, I think. I get home and decide on a compromise—I remove the ring and slide it onto my right ring finger. The ring resists more than I expected, but some aggressive twisting and pulling place it squarely past the knuckle and comfortably around the base of my finger. There! A happy place.

By Monday, I hate it. Until you recognize and name the thing, it doesn't exist. But now I can't unsee it. I rub beeswax all over the right hand, pulling, twisting. It won't go. I wrap dental floss round and round the knuckle, strangling my finger to no avail—it's gone bloaty and purple. The poor thing suffocates, blotching as I force it to hold its airless breath. I take awkward breaks to elevate my hand above my head, like it says I should do on Google, so the blood drains back towards my heart.

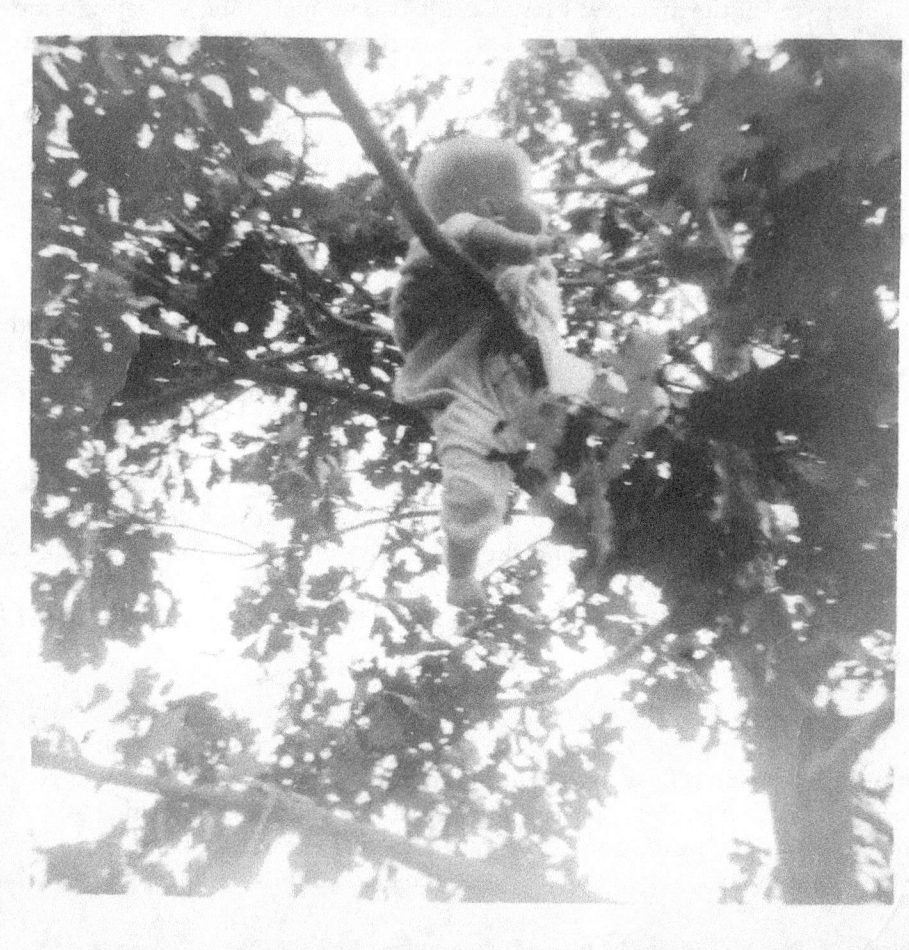

A Doll in the Rain

Nan Ring

Sometimes you will grieve for your old life

Like a child

Finding a beloved doll

Who no longer seems alive.

Who were you then?

What magic held you in a spell that made you smile so,

made you long for so much that you

believed you could have?

What place was this that held you captive in its brief embrace and even now

will not let you go?

The autumn garden is more beautiful in the rain than all the summer sunlit days.

Can it truly be new year?

Can there truly be new life?

Here is the doll forgotten in the garden in the rain, heavy and soaked through

Like a newly planted seed.

Nan Ring, *Doll in the Rain*, gelatin silver print, 4" x 4", 1965

My Stomach Hurts

Annisia Martinez

My stomach hurts.

I am chill

I am hopeful

I am eating at the palm of your hand

I am dumb

I was told

Through side eyes

I am embarrassing

Because

I give it time

I give it head

I get in return

Always enough

But never with love

And

I am

Giving up

I am crying

I ate too much

I ate too much

He's a Scorpio!
Annisia Martinez

He's a Scorpio!

When he kisses my hand!

"According to this source I'm manipulative
And you're attention seeking."
So, I kiss his hand.

"What's your moon?"

A smirk
But
We move onto the next tab
More hopeful.

Darshita Jain
Parley

I don't want my kids growing up in Chicago
I don't want my kids growing up
I   want my kids   in Chicago
I   want   Chicago
                kids   in Chicago
            my kids   in Chicago
I   want   kids growing up
                         Chicago
I
I   want
          kids
            growing up
            growing
                   Chicago
    my

Stop Looking Over Your Shoulder

there is no attack
no slicing the clouded faith shrouded sheath (romance)
is not dead i am here and alive - you - still hiding
a blade under your skin for a day i sin
you open and try to cut me in
uneven pieces of us floating in space
oil pouring black dirtying the mirror
Our sea runs red. At least you extracted the blade.

but its equally true of parking, or hunting, or wishing you could take it back.

when it was, as it is

(4)

Machines
Shou Jie Eng

1551.

Write to you as if the maestro is not watching.

As if he is not in the pen, the ink, the paper that I write to you with. As if he is not already everywhere in my life *(the life that I have, after you sent me away, a boy, to his workshop)*. As if I do not, each morning, see him in his study, his head an arrow out of line from his spine, over the sketches of the basilica of Santa Maria Novella, his care my care, his love for Alberti *my love for him*. Machines for water and machines of war I draw at his direction, but the mechanisms he loves most are the intricate ones, and these are the ones *I love him too*.

Do you know the sound of a hand-crank

as it turns about its axis, its eccentric creak

the imperfections of the shaft in its housing

my arm the body appear,

revolution after revolution after revolution,

unrelenting? I drew a screw lathe today, mother,

with this same pen and ink *(he already lets me*

write to you) turning in the vertical plane,

the spindle aligned, in the main, with a ray

running from the centre of the earth

perpendicularly to its surface, and upwards

into the ethereal, lunary sphere. The shaft sinks,

plunging till it meets its chock, the headstock

that secures it from the top, the tail from the bottom

to the teeth of the gearing to the winch—

in all this, the missing thing, that the master told me

not to leave in—the body or the beast that drives it all:

the bridle, the blinkers, the bit,

a switch, the lash.

2008.

Write to you as if I am not always watching.

As if my window does not already open onto the yard that your mother so carefully tends. As if I do not see that men have come to dig up a corner of it, next to the porch, where three steps are now too much. As if I do not see your father, whose hands shook even when we first moved in next door, his back stooped with an illness that I recognised immediately, his feet the shuffle of dragging time.

No one hands him the leaf-blower any more

after years of pretending with the old mower turned off

your mother working the grass behind. *Your father fell today,*

I say, and immediately all this I see:

the hot field stone, the bleached grass

your mother stooping over him, her body

cupping, straining to help him sit up,

the ambulance people, a chair in the shade

a walker with tennis balls for feet

a wheelchair, scooter, wheelchair again

his balled foot trailing, having slid

between plate and ground.

One morning the workmen come to unearth your mother's garden as she brings them iced water. They lay the edging for the concrete pad, tracking chalky marks on her drive; they arrive again with their white boxes and the white lift deck *(hydraulic pump motor, pump and opposite side cylinders, control pad)* and when they leave I write to you again to say that *I have not seen your father in days.*

2016.

Write to you as if you were not also watching.

One handler nearly slips the casket

our eyes get large

scissor lift

furnace mouth

the flange tips

as the rollers engage our cries

a body, at last, *alive.*

The Brown Stain Bleeds

Dana Brinson

The brown stain bleeds

Remnant of the open pen dropped carelessly to the blanket.

Spill some ink, spirit says.

Pour it out.

Speak your words and our words and **THE** words.

You came to me in a dream last night, Dad

Flesh torn from your face and one eye removed, you said you did this to yourself, willingly.

What does that mean?

Am I to follow your lead? Dig under the skin? Reveal the secrets?

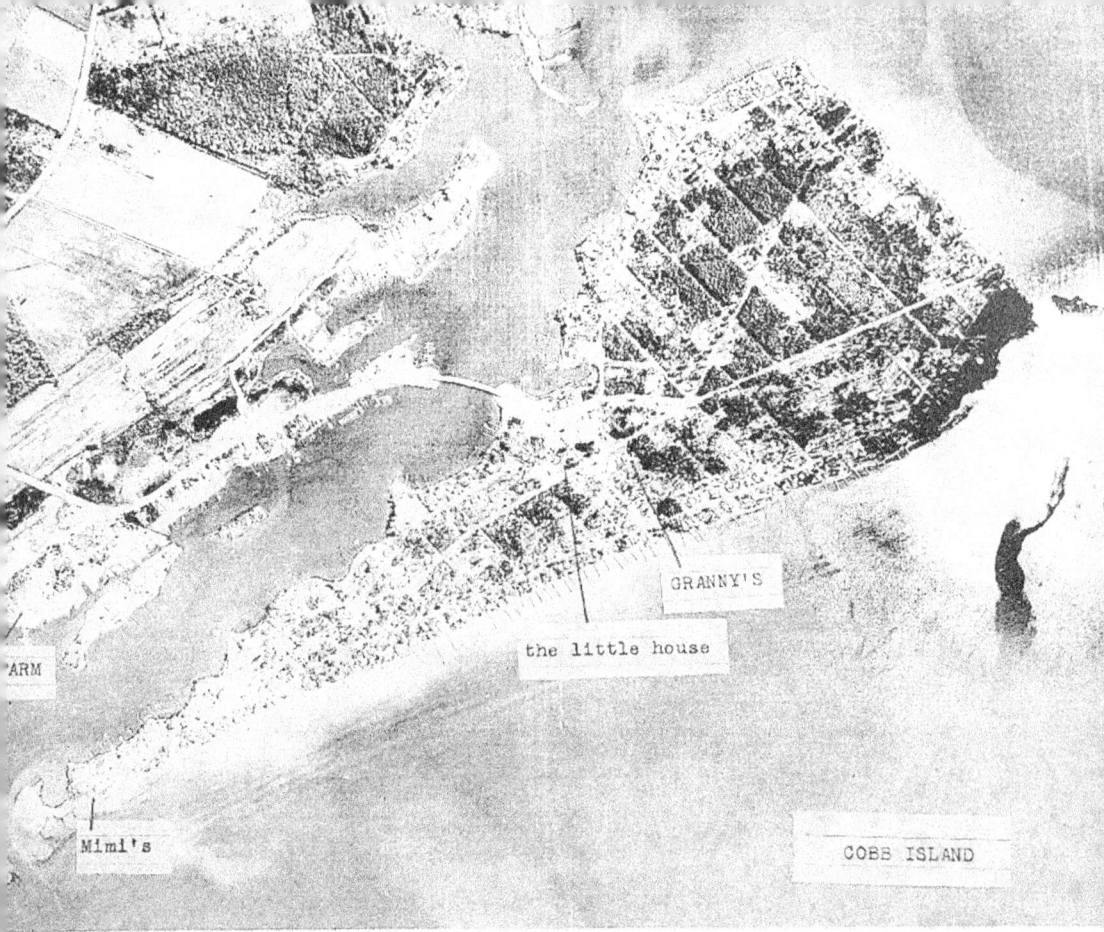

GRANNY'S

the little house

ARM

Mimi's

COBB ISLAND

Mom, on her death bed, wanted to share your deepest secret. The one you refused to let her tell us in life.

And we refused to let her speak it. Wanting to honor you.

But isn't the purpose of the death bed to be a time for the dying to release their burdens?

Aren't we supposed to play the role of witness? To carry on those burdens for them?

By honoring you, did we—my sister and me—dishonor our mother?

It was reflex, really, because she shared so many precious secrets in her life. Unwilling to consider others' needs over her own taste for juicy gossip.

We resisted out of habit. Denying her worst impulses, which she failed to shed, even in her dying moments. Selfish to the end.

But in denying her that release and one last thrill of sharing someone's sweet secret, we lost our last chance to know you more fully.

Funny and boisterous and kind, you were a chimera, an enigma, a mystery. Never going too deep, you seemed content.

But learning, late in your life, that there was this secret that you did not want mom to share. That you got visibly upset at the hint that she was about to reveal it, makes me yearn for closeness with you. To go deep and ask all the questions I was afraid to ask or didn't think to ask, or thought you wouldn't answer.

You were funny and boisterous and kind. But in some ways I never knew you.

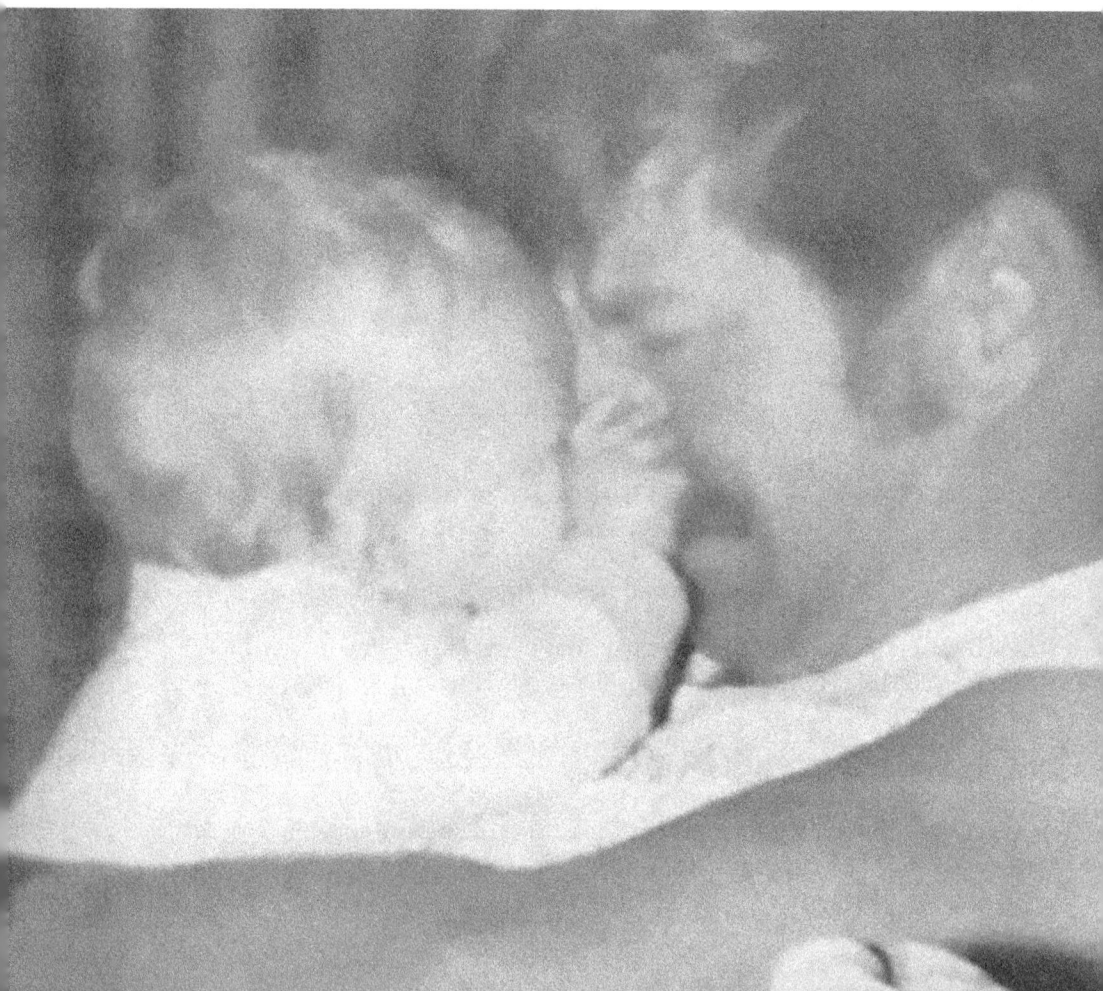

What made you weep at night? What scared you when the darkness crept in? What did you reveal to mom, the world's worst secret keeper that she ACTUALLY kept secret until death she parted?

How many secrets died with grandparents and greats and great great greats? What do I carry of those rusted fragments in my blood of their blood and bone of their bones?

What?

I can't get the image out of my head of your face, torn open, looking calmly at me as if in no pain, with no worries at the disfiguration. Was it a message for me? To spill my blood to remember you?

Spill the ink. Soak it through and through.

The night before, I met mom and her brother Jack in a dream. Both departed, sitting at a card table under a massive interstate overpass. Sitting at the table was Aunt Bernie. You had made a place for her, but she's still here. She's coming soon, I think, and these two are the welcoming party.

They are ready when she is.

The land, the farm, the marina—sells on Friday—after more than half a century in our family's hands. Dearly won and cheaply lost, this land took more than it gave from all of us.

My grandmother's dreams my grandfather's schemes my aunts and uncles shed their fair share of tears and sweat and blood on that land. Some from hard work. Others in fights. And one, my cousin JJ, just 41 years old, shed his life there. Found in the river. A mystery that won't be unraveled because the world deemed him unworthy of the sustained interest.

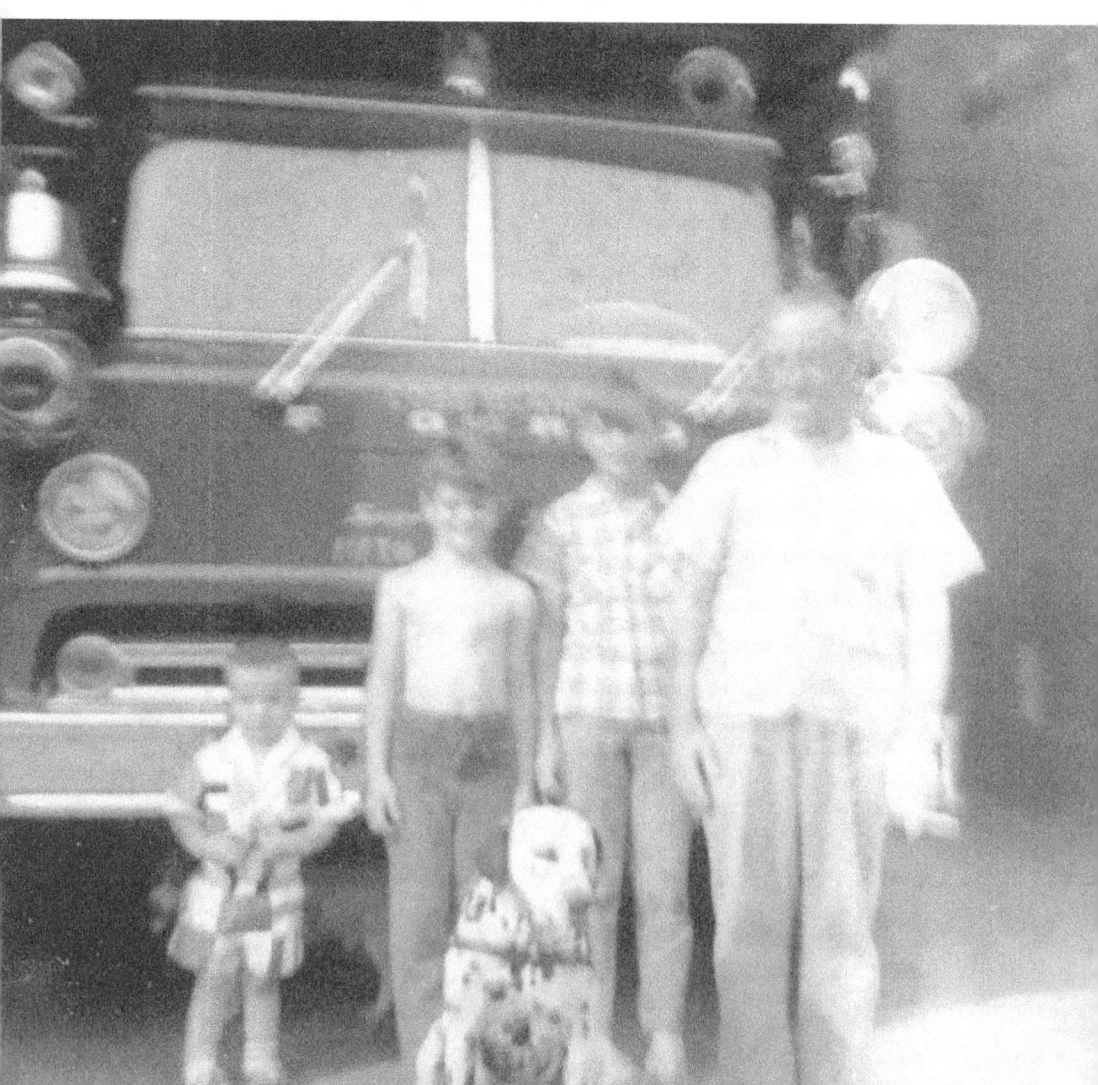

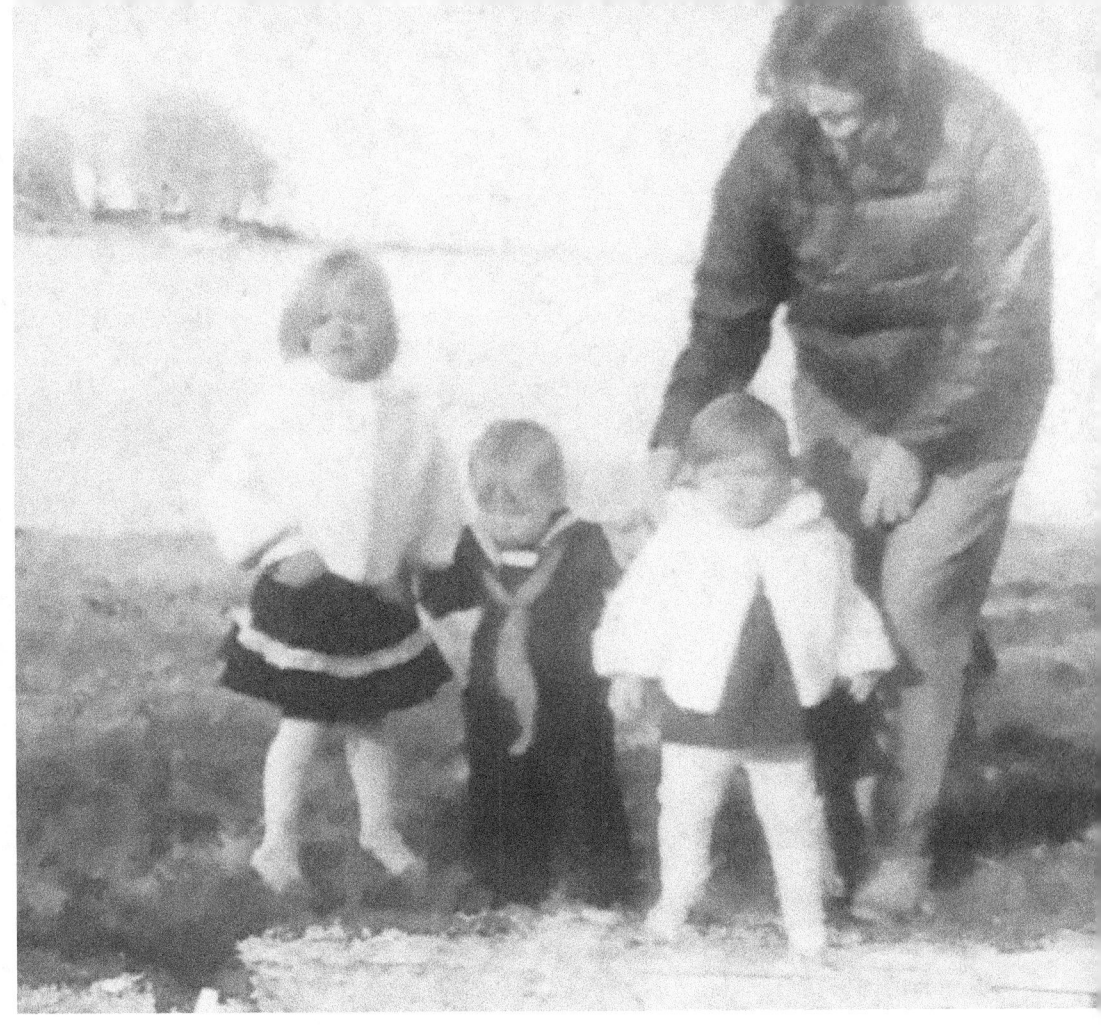

So the land is released. And so, too, soon, will be my aunt.

Leaving only Spider. The least of them all to be the last.

The key. That will lock the door behind him when he leaves.

The matrilineal line is dead. My sister and I have killed it good.

But my grandmother has great-grandchildren who will carry on this blood of her blood and bone of her bone and the losses and fears and violence and labor and sweat and laughter. They carry my grandfather, too. They will never know them or perhaps even of them. Because their father is gone in the river and the rest of us scattered to the wind.

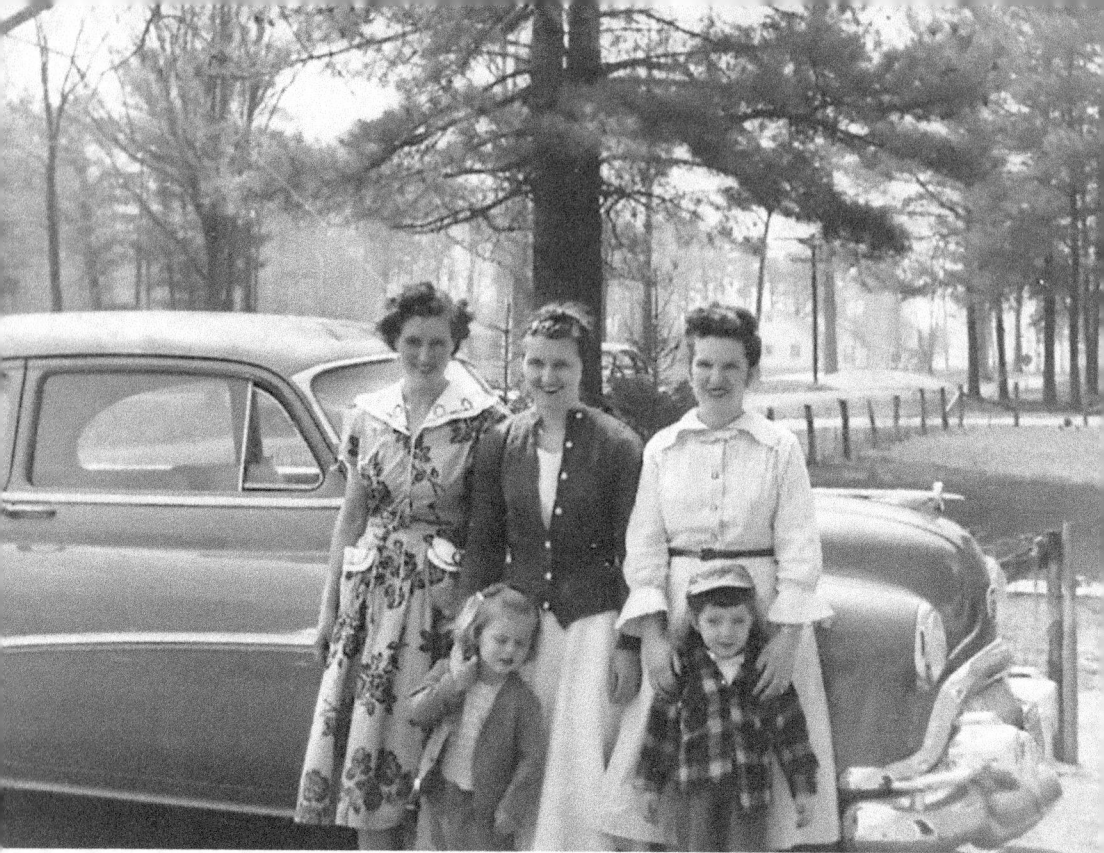

They won't know of summer days on the farm, Potomac rising and falling as the crabs spread on the news-papered table.

Small bottles of Bud and dishes of butter.

The mumbled words around dangling cigarettes.

Feeling flush with the heat of the day and the alcohol and the joy of being alive in this one perfect moment.

They won't know oysters grilled in a World War II bomb casing, rusted nearly through now but dragged from the river, placed there by Dahlgren during end-less testing, and pulled up by one of the watermen in my family, and made into something that prepared sustenance for us.

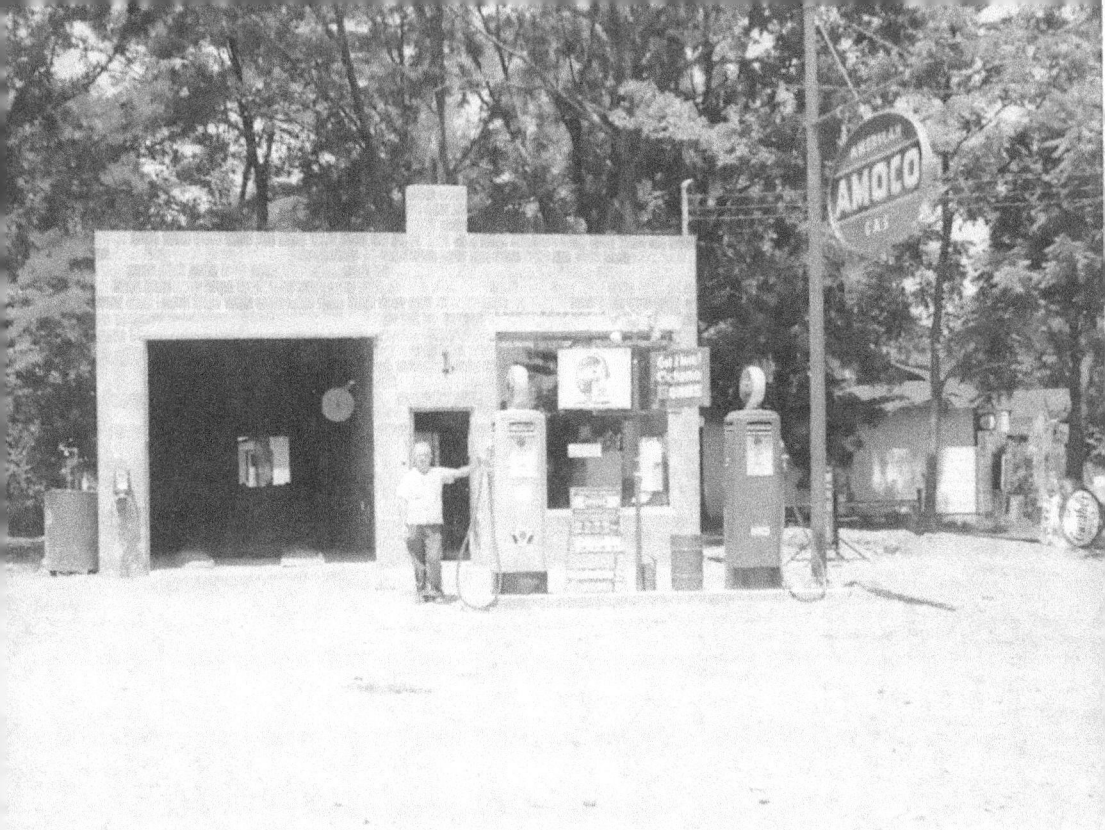

I cry the tears of the men spiraling back generations carrying empty jars. Dry.

No tears shed, carried within and packaged neatly and passed along. For the next generation to tend to. Or ignore.

Here I am at the end of the line, with all these tears to shed that cannot be shed in a lifetime.

Dinesen said salt water can cure anything—sweat, tears or the sea.

Saltwater

How many tears did you shed out on the river, for no one to see?

How much of you remains there?

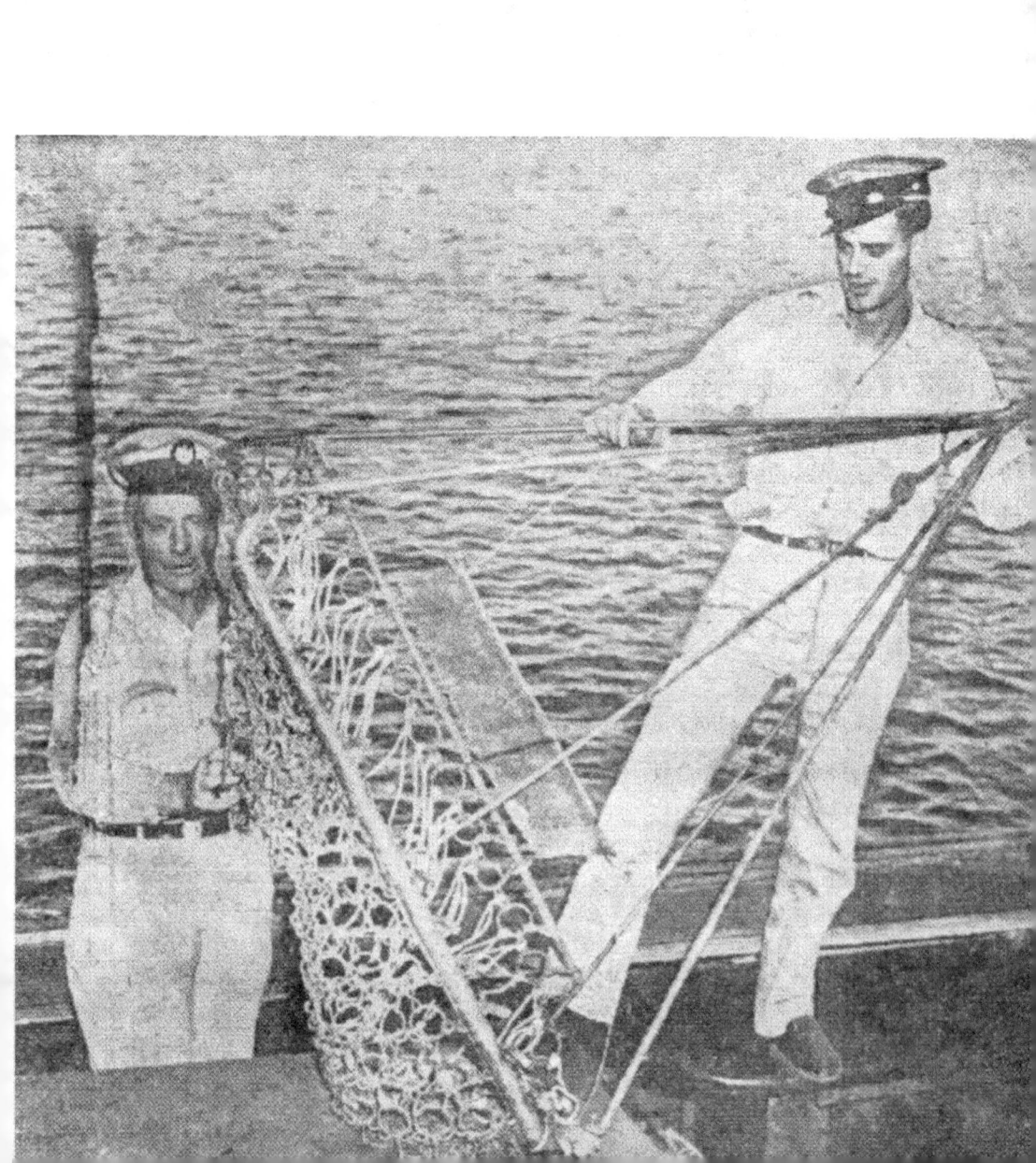

Grang, you fired a machine gun once to protect Maryland oyster beds from Virginia men stealing from them. I don't know if that was the first time you fired a machine gun in the line of service. You were in Italy after the war, and may never have had cause for it there.

Oysters connected me with mom when she lived next door. In her last years here, we ate so many delicious dozens. And we laughed at how the local North Carolina boy pronounced the Wicomico. But we knew. Southern Maryland girls for three centuries.

Our grandmothers go back that far. What remains of our mother land, England, we think, in our bones if we are three centuries here?

How can I carry these stories on my own? No child to share them with? No one to pass on the pain and relieve myself?

Who will witness me on my death bed?

Who will surround me with love?

How will I ever cry enough tears? This terrible obligation you left to me.

How can I be so proud of you and ashamed? Moments in the mind's eye bring back fun and fear, laughter and anger, hope and desperation.

Scrambling and enough.

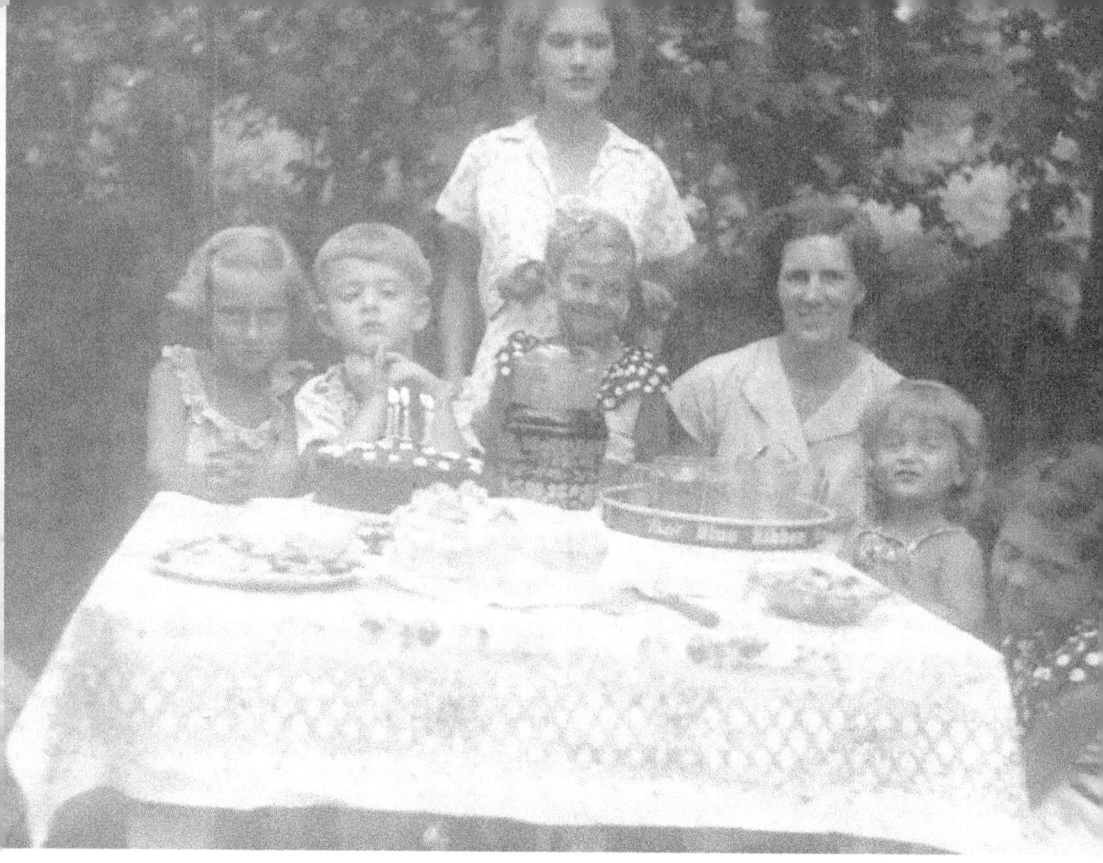

You each had careless natures toward your longevity but a taste for life in this moment that was unparalleled.

You are me. I am you. I am of you. I am in you. You are in me. We are in the river. We are in the ground.

We take flight like the osprey.
Stand still like the crane.   Float gracefully like the swan.

We pinch like the crab our necks and arms boiled red in the sun. Faces lined with work and worry.

I never felt a part. I never felt apart.

Shame and satisfaction at the same.

The river, the river, the river branches flows and meets at the Island. Potomac Wicomico Neale Sound. A triangle like the one in Bermuda, where things got lost never to be found.

A home, a store, a restaurant, a garage, a firehouse, a home. You built it and lost it. Grew it and destroyed it. Made it and unmade it. Just as with yourselves.

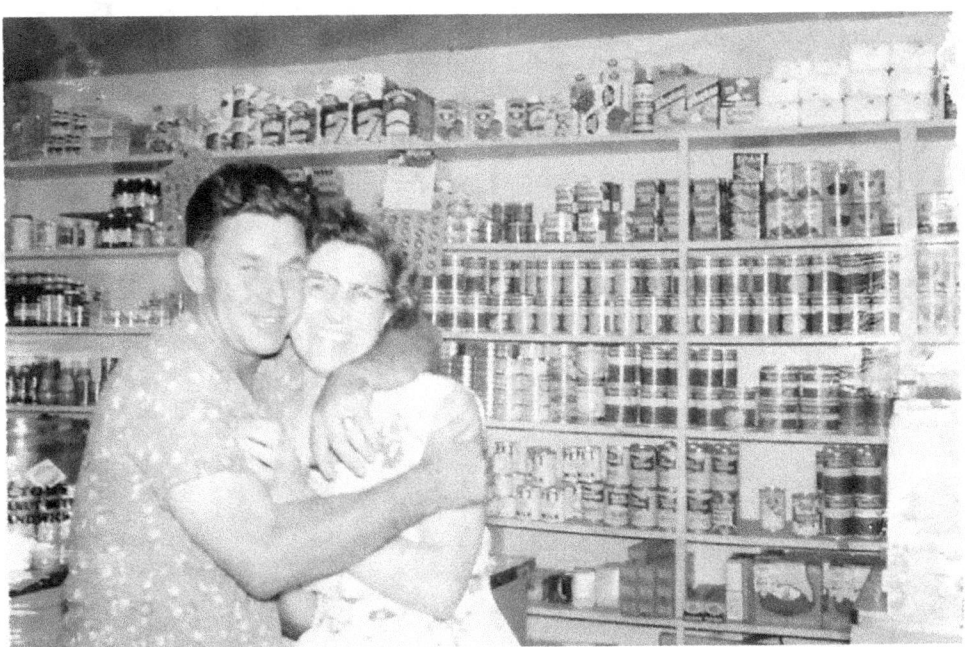

And here I am, having made nothing of consequence. No building standing because I willed it to be. No business built that makes or fixes things or feeds people or comes in emergencies to provide help and consolation.

I don't have a real job.

I have the realest job. The one the captures your stories and puts them down. Spills the ink for you.

What you made was rent asunder. By time and carelessness and wantonness and drunkenness and laziness and fear.

What I make could last forever. Or perhaps never be read.

My mother was five when she walked the Island with her best friend Barb. Peeking and sneaking and looking for snakes and frogs. Finding crabs on the pilons holding up the bridge that connected this little land and the big land beyond. She grew there, in the center of that Island surrounded by cousins and aunts and uncles and grandparents. Rooted. But unsure and perhaps unloved. Or not loved enough.

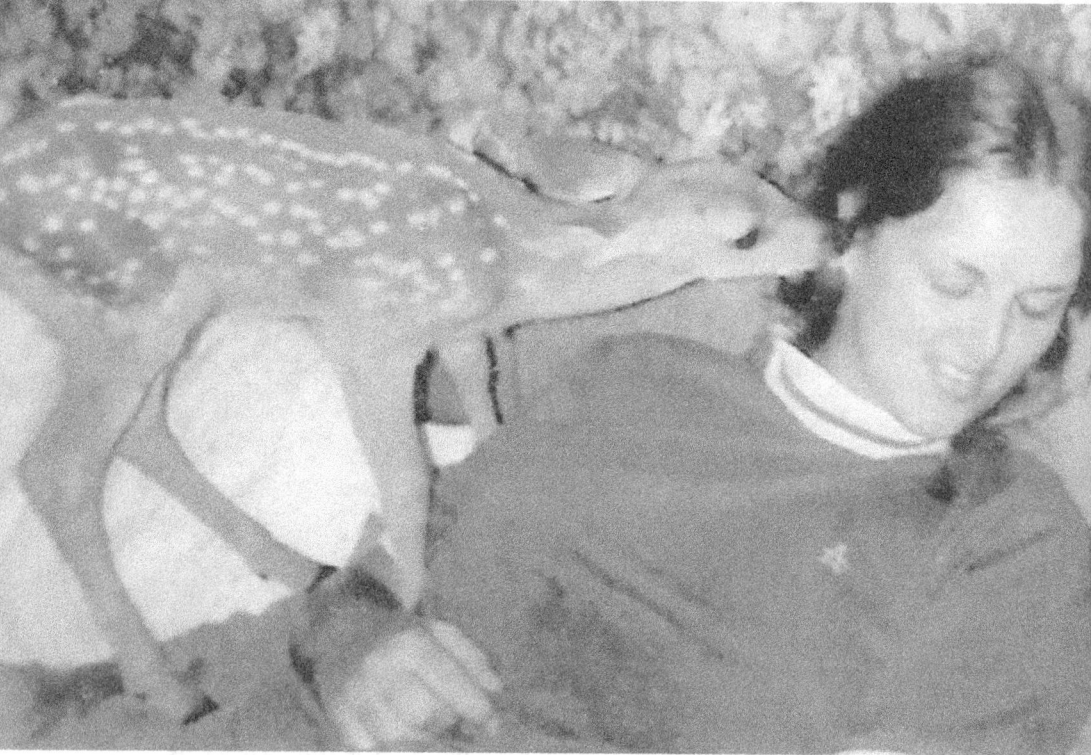

So she grew to love herself in a way that benign and lazy narcissists do. The fun kind, if you don't have to be raised by her.

But she grew up rooted. Knowing who she was. She was a Southern Maryland girl. Daughter of people who scraped by, who worked hard, who fought. Who always had another seat at the table for a wayward soul. Who always had animals show up to find a home. Monkeys, a deer, a duck that chased cars with the dogs. A tiny home before tiny homes were desired. Cramped and uneven. Enough.

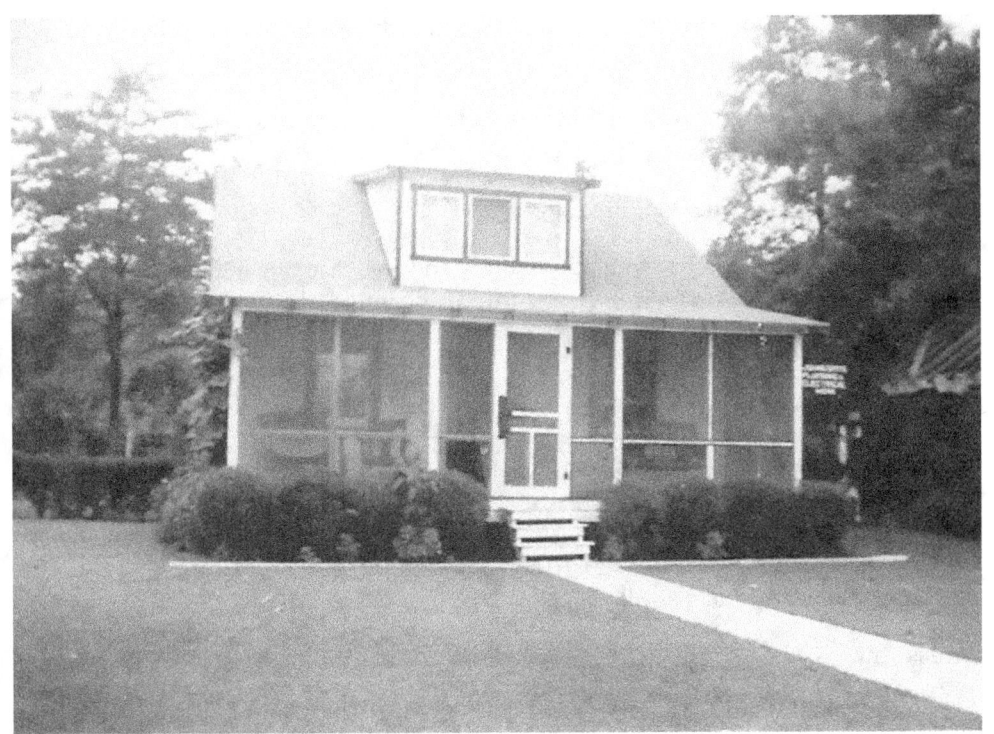

Aunt Cassie who didn't have kids or a home or much of anything beyond the skill
to keep her cigarette balanced and bobbing in the corner of her mouth   growing
an impressive ash. She sang Babyface in her gravelly voice and showed up at a
cousin's or nephew's or your house and stayed for a while—to be fed and housed.

And she would steal your food to take to the next house who needed her as much as she needed them.

I know Aunt Cassie only through mom's stories. She carried those stories to me. Fragments. Slivers. Precious.

No more stories to come. You are all gone.

Except Bernie who cannot remember stories and they are not hers to tell since she was only unfortunate enough to marry into this family.

Spider though, he has plenty of stories. Tales to tell. Laughs to share.

Do I crave stories enough to call him?

Will he make me miss you more? Or awaken the shame?   Both are likely.

Carrying your stories, spilling your ink, getting beneath your skin has me cold and under a blanket and grabbing an extra sweater on this July morning. Carrying the stories of the dead exacts a toll.

I miss you.

How can you all be gone?

How can that have happened?

At four decades someone should have people still. A sister and cousin remain of that clan. My people.

And Spider.

But for how long?

What will I wish I had asked if I had had the chance?

The moment he is dead is when that question will come.

Finality opens curiosity that can never be satisfied.

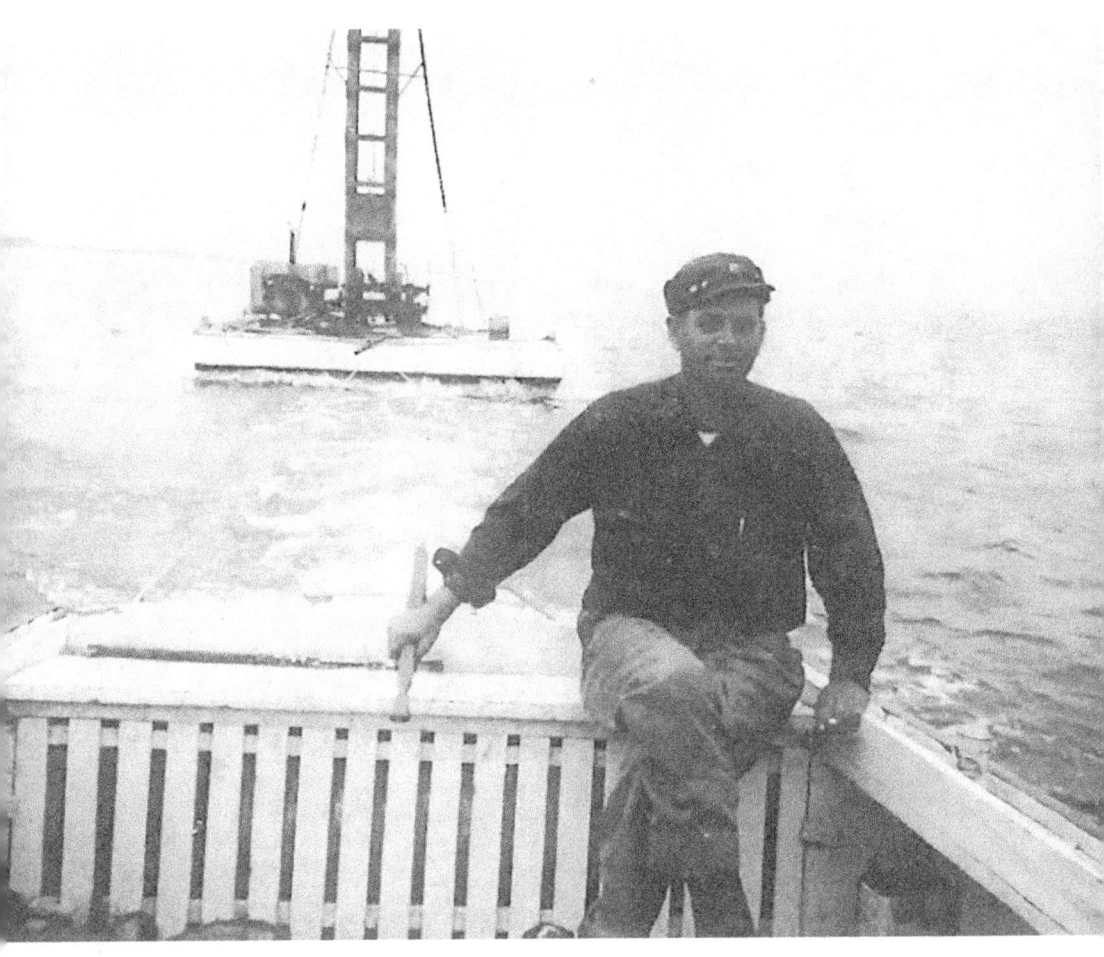

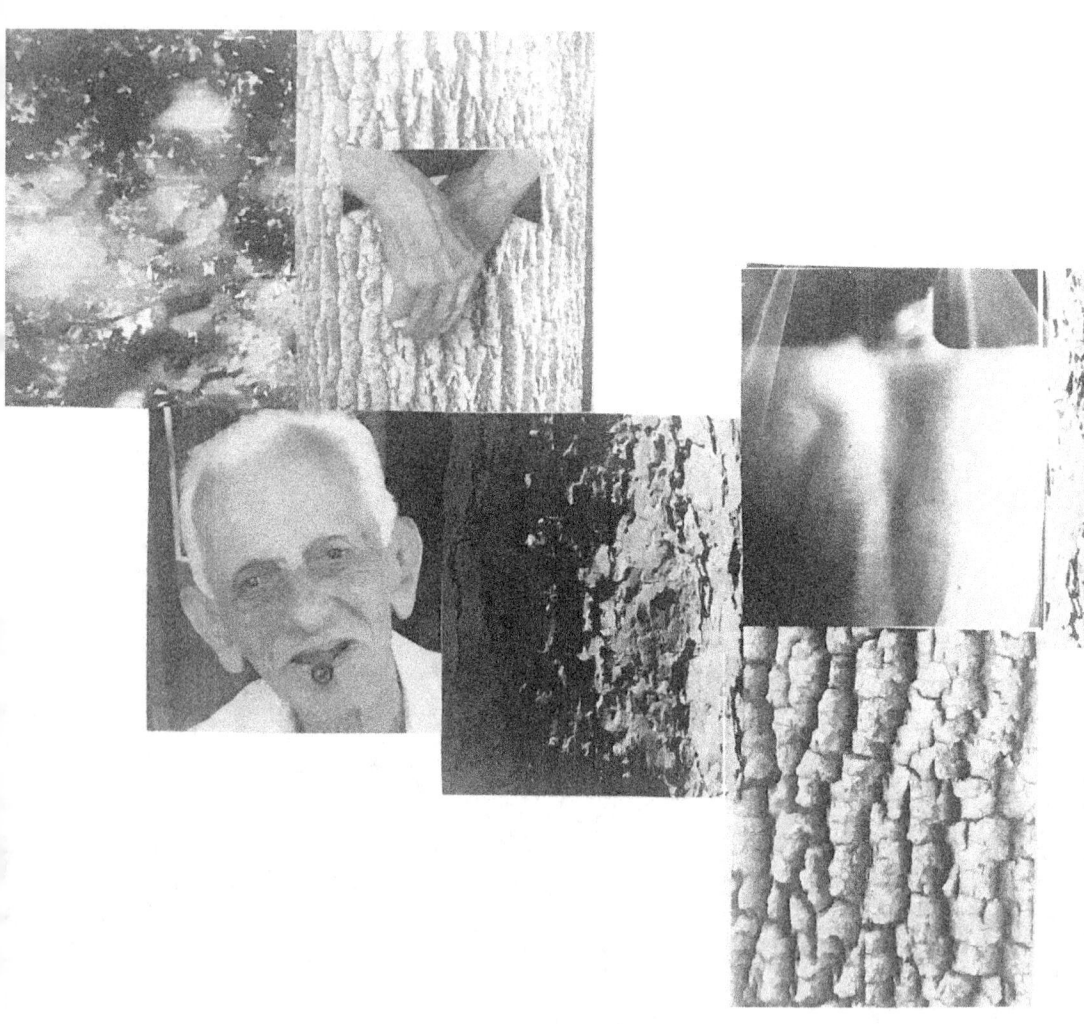

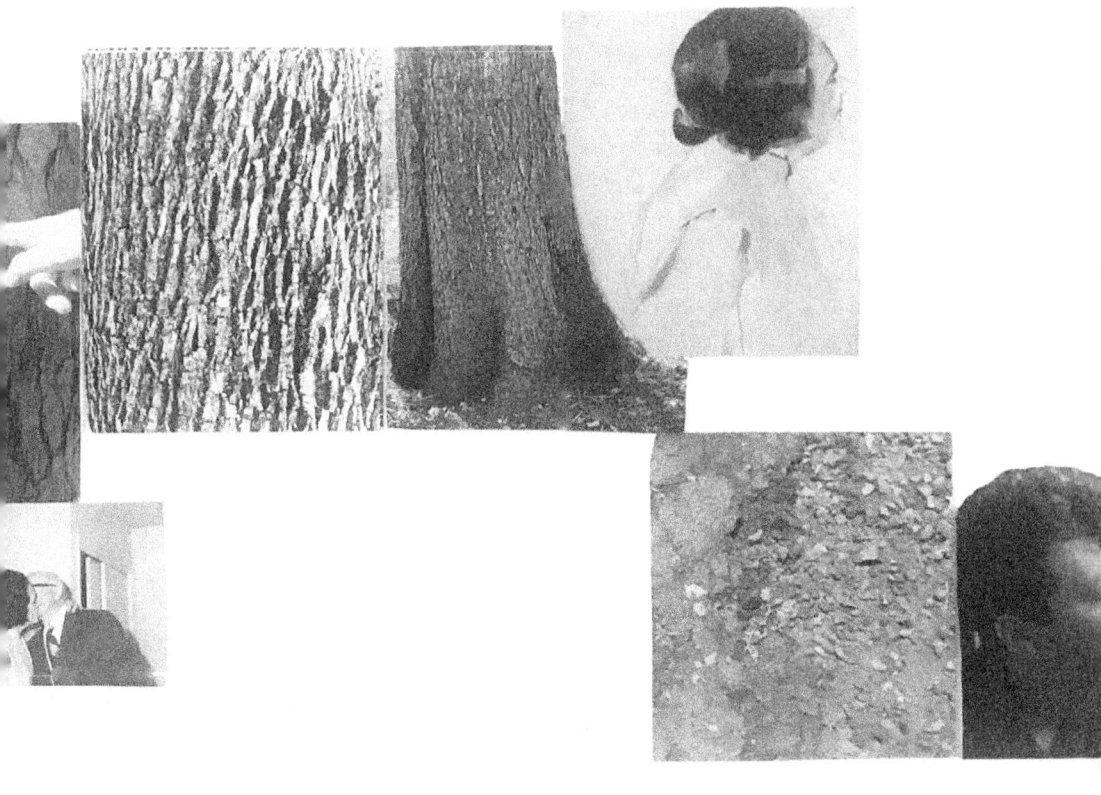

Elephantine

Nan Ring

1.

My heavy wrinkled dress fits like netting draped over soft mud. The weight of it tugging through, a gravity, no discernible difference between wearer and the worn. Wrinkles keep elephants cooler, for longer, than if they had smooth skin, thermo-regulating through evaporative cooling (Supplementary Videos 1, 2.) An old reel of me at 50, after the divorce, dancing at my niece's wedding. Mists fill the crags, lifting the heat of long told stories. Whorls of eddying water pool in the browned grass where we mud-wallow. Cepheus glittering in the night sky. On stick legs, old grasshoppers tat their chirping lace as the heavy wrinkles sink into the crevices, smelling of millennia and heart smoke, of clothes left too long in a trunk. Would that I could try them on, wear them to dance again, strip them off at will, releasing stingers. Instead they fit too well, a dumpling skin encased in steam, and my arms cramp in an X over my chest, trying to remove them over my head. It's too late; winter is arriving fast, and I am no calf. I come into my elephant skin, filling it up, spilling stars in sparkler fire.

2.

Mud-wallowing. Slathering mud in the intricate crevices, spraying it down with cool still water, painting with mud again. A life's work, paid through the nose.

3.

Listen. Reams of skin–fine, smooth tapestries in feather-smooth threads–can be bought. Sellers in bodies of blue sky and clouds cut the reams with long, sharp incisors.

Preceding pages:
Nan Ring, *Elephantine Collage*, digital and silver gelatin photographs and paintings on paper, 16" x 60", 2020

4.

Photographs searched in Google images. Click. Loading pages. Human
hand cursor grabs and drags. "Beauty shots" of elephant skin photographed
close up. Human with trunk for a nose labeled birth defect. Elephant with
trunk draped over her calf. Human embracing another. Woman with heavily
wrinkled skin. The Hulk. Human being pointing a loaded gun at another.
Human being pointing a rifle with cocked trigger at an elephant. Human
being's airbrushed photo of another human being. Obese child. Albino.
Ancient hand-inked papyrus, rolling pin smoothed (memory. surfacing: a
transparent scrim over the screen, my mother's arthritic hands in mountain
ranges of elephant-knuckles showing me how to roll dough.) Tatted up young
human with sleeves of curling ink. Surfacing, surfacing, memories overlay
the screen images, old slides projected in the space between my eyes and the
monitor: your face, beloved to me, with the rings under your eyes that you
tell me you hate on our second date, my aunt's profile at 90, the crumbling
windowsills on my enclosed porch that I can't bring myself to scrape and
paint.

5.

Mud runs in veins of earth, shallows, seeps up in the dry beds of rivers. I
remember my sister teaching me to wash our camp plates with mud in a
stream. Elephant skin is clean, creased from rolling, mud-filled and mud-
loved, rolling over a curvilinear interior, storied, danced in, worn-worn. Slept
in like sweat soaked dresses worn to satisfied exhaustion. Slept in, sleep-lived.
Sleep-lived backwards, old souls coming into innocence, rolled back like film
reels in reverse, images ending at their beginnings, absorbed into a night sky
of scratched cellulose acetate negatives. Cepheus, dead not-dead in his old
skin, lived backward to his calf-self, reborn star by star forever in an interior
of night sky. From sleep to burning ever-alive constellation, I awake. I awake,
look up in the middle of the night, wrinkled and damp, astonished that I have
lived and loved, even now, in this priceless, one of a kind garment. Only one,
my old and owned and only skin.

Land Use Excursions, Revisited

Christine Lorenz

In the summer of 1997, I was looking for somewhere to go. I had just finished my MFA, and it didn't look like there was going to be enough work to keep me in Santa Barbara for very long. If Southern California didn't work out, I might go back to Ohio, or possibly someplace I'd never been before. The previous two years had made for a lot of time taking pictures, looking at lot of photography from history, and thinking about how people processed their experiences through the pictures they made. So whenever there was time for a road trip, I would take cameras along. None of these cameras were very high quality,

and some of them were literally toys. The low-tech styles that the cameras brought to the pictures seemed to me to make them more human, to each have their own distinctive voice. The authoritative tone of documentary photography seemed to me presumptuous, rendering declarative views of things-as-they-are, sharp and clear and undisputable. So much more seemed possible.

Lucky for me, the Center for Land Use Interpretation had organized a series of bus tours to selected exurbs of Los Angeles. The organization was dedicated to exploring the many ways that human endeavors have transformed the

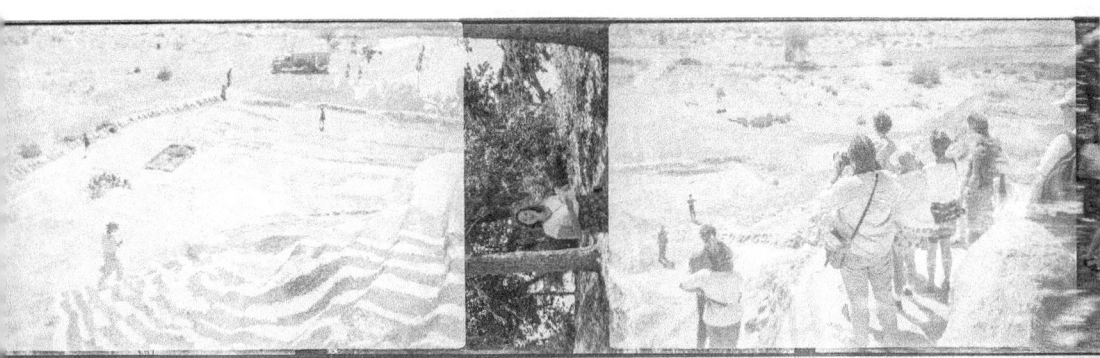

landscape. From military technology to affluence-flaunting leisure to the veneration of aliens, there seemed no end to the purposes the land had been shaped to serve. The tours were hosted by well educated docents, and supplemented by educational films screened on the buses, which, thankfully, were air conditioned. Salvation Mountain and the Salton Sea were part of those tours.

Salvation Mountain is a Mojave desert hillside, on the edge of Slab City, shaped by hand into a monumental testament of faith. It was the project of Leonard Knight, a gregarious visionary who led a monastic life on the site and worked on it continually for over thirty years. Knight built with methods inspired by adobe construction, reinforcing dirt from the site with straw, and sealing it with thick coats of paint. The resulting forms spell out biblical verses, and fill the spaces in between with colorful flowers and flowing painted streams. The project

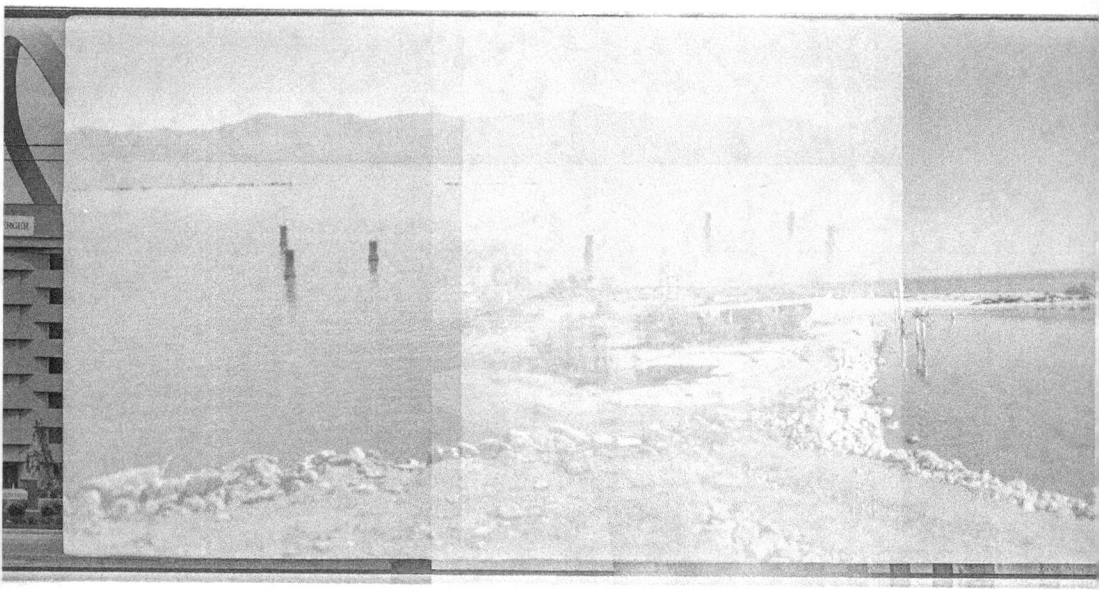

demanded a continuous supply of paint: thousands of gallons of it, much of it donated piecemeal by visitors. By the time of Knight's death in 2013, it was as tall as a three story building and more than 100 feet long. Salvation Mountain stands today in technicolor glory, thanks to the ongoing labor of volunteers and philanthropic support. It's an ongoing battle against erosion and the bleaching rays of the sun. In the extremes of the desert climate, there's only one way to keep the mountain intact: paint, and more paint, year after year.

It's a short drive from Salvation Mountain to reach the Salton Sea, a broad expanse that stands hundreds of feet below sea level. In geological terms, the meanderings of the Colorado River have influenced the form of this region over time. In the early 1950s, it was a dry desert basin, but industrial-scale irrigation of the Imperial Valley rapidly transformed

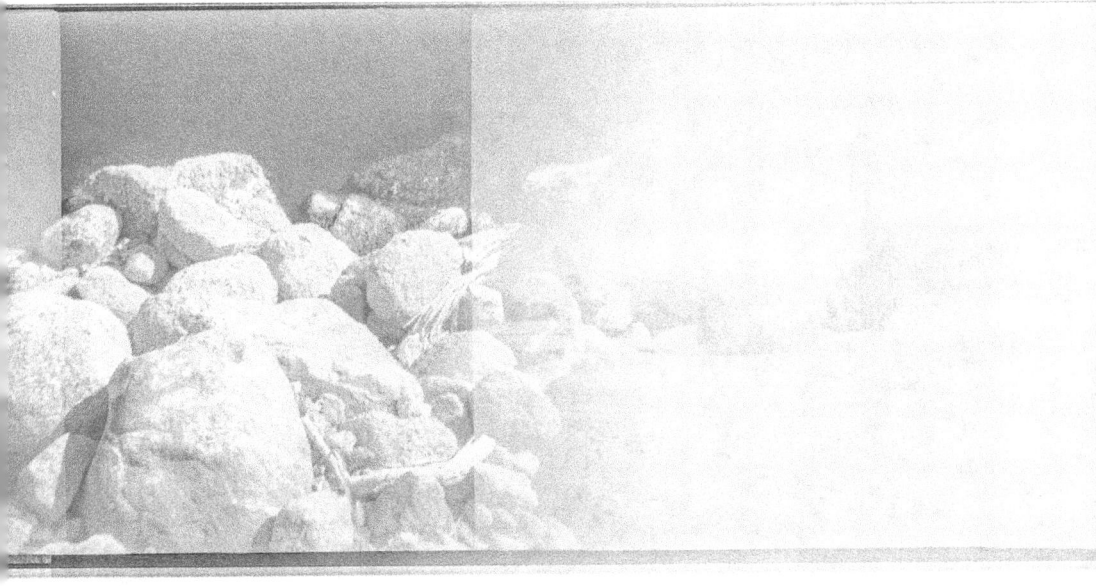

it into the largest inland body of water in California. Chemical salts from agricultural runoff made for an unusual water ecosystem with staggering algae blooms. Tilapia were introduced in attempt to control the algae, but they started a boom and bust population cycle of their own, leaving rings of desiccated, salt-encrusted skeletons behind as the Salton Sea gradually contracted. It has no remaining natural tributaries, and the sun and heat are merciless. As a result, the chemical content of the slowly evaporating body of water has become increasingly concentrated. The air carries with it the fine dust that the shrinking lake leaves behind, raising the rates of asthma and cancers in the remaining local population. Despite the contamination, over 380 species of birds are known to depend on the Salton Sea as a resting point on the Pacific Flyway.

The American drive to think big and build bigger is by no means limited to the desert, as evidenced by the story of the Longaberger Building, which rose in the heartland of Newark, Ohio, minutes from the town where I grew up.

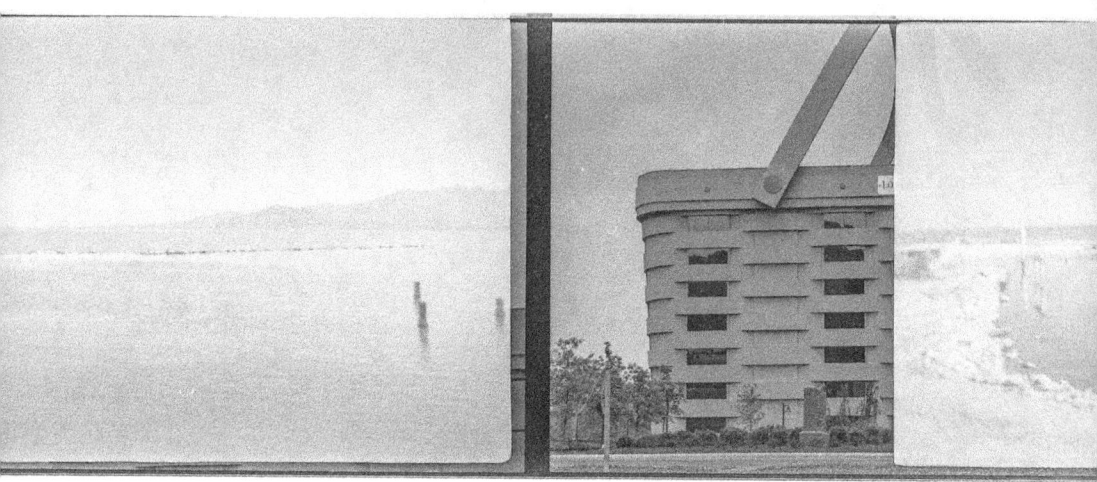

The Longaberger company caught the eyes of the world when they built their Home Office as a seven-story replica of their signature product: the Market Basket[1]. The company had been a major employer in the area for decades, hiring thousands to weave decorative baskets from strips of maple, creating variations on a style that went back generations. Enthusiastic collectors paid status prices to acquire their wares through a network of home-based sales representatives.

Their seasonal lines of nostalgic décor skyrocketed in popularity through the 1990s, making Longaberger a household name. They continued to expand, enlisting tens of thousands of sellers around the world, and taking on increasing debt in the years that followed. An outside investment group eventually acquired Longaberger, making them the star of their lineup of multi-level marketing companies. Within five years, all of those companies were bankrupt. The name

[1] The building was famous well before it opened, and people with an interest in buildings instantly pegged it as a "duck." Fans of American vernacular architecture will recognize this term from *Learning from Las Vegas*, by Robert Venturi, Denise Scott Brown and Steven Izenour. The authors found two significant approaches to the design of buildings."Decorated sheds" were shaped in nondescript ways, and relied on signage to alert passersby to their function. Certain other buildings announced their purpose through the shape of the buildings themselves, and these were called "ducks," deriving from a

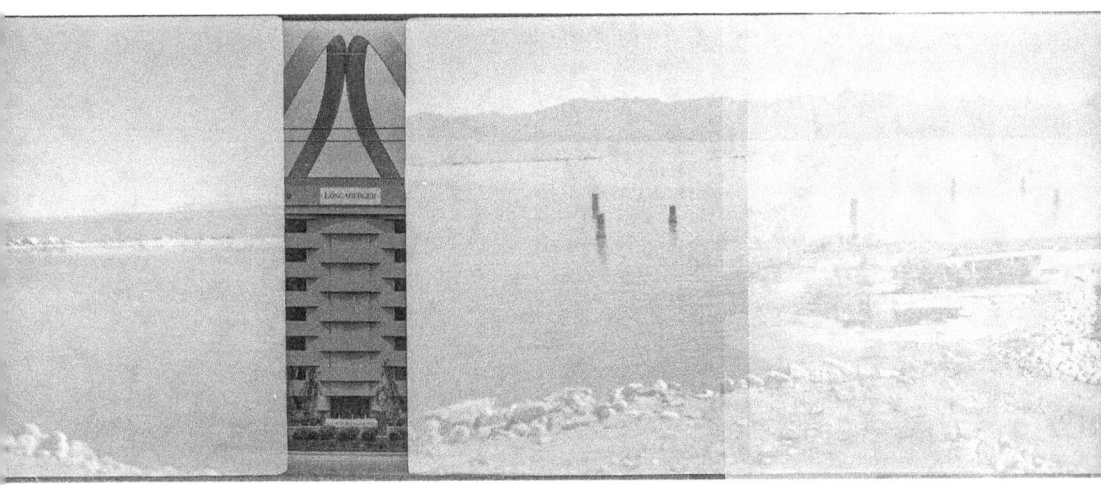

was sold again, along with the factory and all of their real estate assets. Twenty years after the basket building's opening, it was bought at auction by a real estate developer. There have been announcements that it would be converted into a luxury hotel, but a look around at the economically distressed region would make that idea seem as out of context as the building itself. Today the building stands vacant over a parking lot overrun with weeds. But you can buy those traditional baskets again, in freshly updated

styles. An artisanal quantity of them are made in Ohio, and sold on QVC. On social media, brand ambassadors for the Longaberger name stage photographs of their collections from their own homes, all across the United States, Europe, and Asia.

Min-Yi Lin came to the United States as a graduate student, and presented his installation "Dwellings" after completing his degree in ceramics at the Univerity of Calfornia, Santa Barbara. Lin's sculptural

farmstand building the authors once encountered, which sold ducks and duck eggs, and was literally shaped like ... a duck. This pairing of architecture types still reverberates in certain circles. Curious readers are encouraged to dive down that rabbit hole online; they will find that Googling the terms "learning from Las Vegas" and "duck" will lead them to numerous articles illustrated with photographs of the Longaberger building.

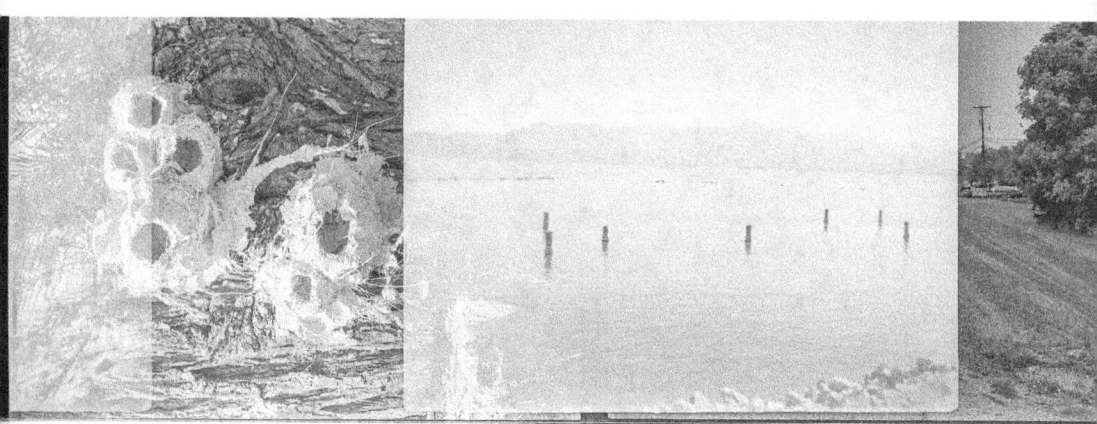

forms were inspired by non-human builders: birds that weave nests, moths that spin cocoons, wasps that house colonies in paper orbs filled with complex channels. None of these are built to outlast their makers. "Dwellings" was built on a leafy site populated by eucalyptus and live oak, and there were no signs to point out the sculptures. Instead, viewers would meander on their own, gradually finding the oversized spheres woven from pine needles in the branches overhead, and small colonies of unfired clay mounds among rocks. In the crevice of a tree were dozens of plaster and straw niches, resembling the nests that cliff swallows build on the sides of houses when they flock to the neighborhood by the thousands every year. After this exhibition, Lin returned with his family to his native Taiwan. As intended, the sculptures were at the mercy of the elements, and most were dismantled when the exhibition ended. The eucalyptus groves in this region are known around the world as gathering sites for Monarch butterflies. Their location is one of extraordinary beauty, and as a result, the sites are under constant threat of acquisition by real estate developers. This kind of habitat loss is a primary reason for the plummet of Monarch populations in recent years. A trust funded by the city has purchased acres of wooded lots, like the one that once held Min-Yi Lin's installation, in effort to insure that in this place at least, swallows and butterflies can find refuge on their migratios. on their migrations.

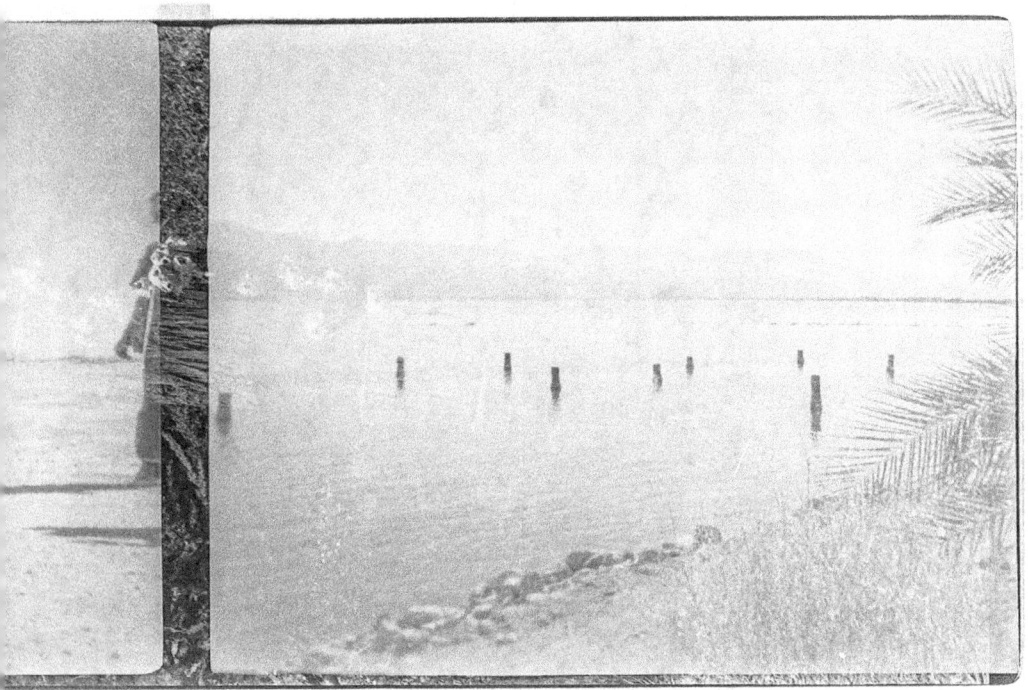

I came back to these photos in the late spring of 2020, a time of fragmentation and uncertainty. Time itself seemed to have slipped out of all sense of structure, expanding and contracting, beyond control. In the early months of the pandemic, the luckiest among us were spending our suddenly undifferentiated time at home, and it seemed like a good enough time to dig up old projects that had been put away unfinished. A lot of people were talking about these projects in terms of nostalgia. But when I looked at these photographs again, I wasn't seeing a time I wished I could return to. I saw something like time folding in on itself, and from this point of view, it's hard to see any kind of moving-on as even possible. In America, we've never been quite able to accept that the past isn't the past, that it's not even over. It's hard to feel ready for what comes next; we've been wrong about the future before. One thing we can't deny, now, is that there will be no fresh start. We built things that we can't simply leave behind.

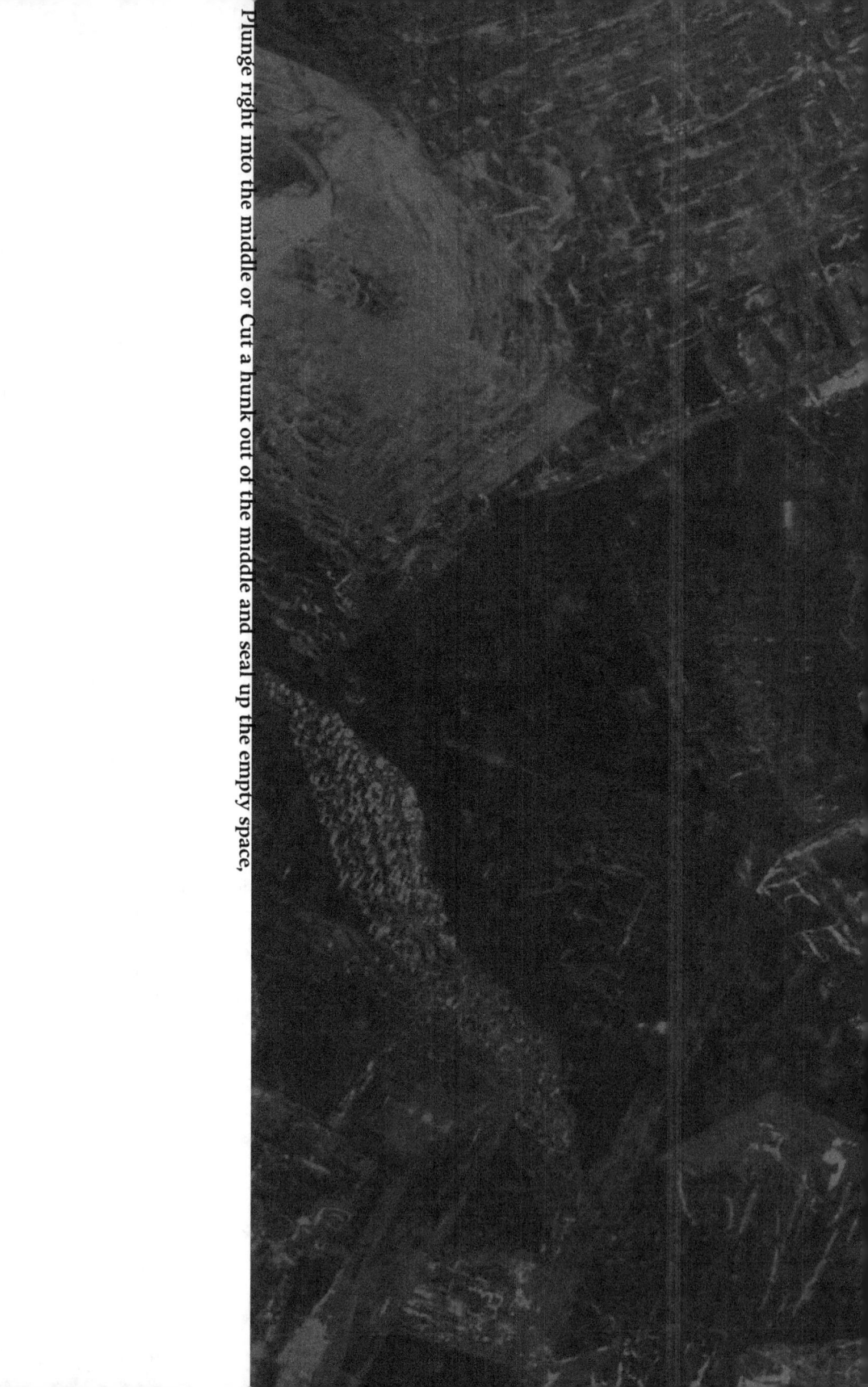

Plunge right into the middle or Cut a hunk out of the middle and seal up the empty space,

now/rupture

(5)

I leave at eleven in the morning, and return at midnight

Shou-Jie Eng

The email arrives, its subject line immediately visible. The polling date is one day earlier than I had thought, and I spend Wednesday morning looking up trains all over again. The blue of my calendar blurs into the blue of Google Maps into the blue of the transit authority's trip planner as I tab between browser windows, mapping, experimentally, a set of possible itineraries. It was a five-hour journey each way in 2015, and I am grateful that this time, at least, it is only four. I remember a former colleague, an American, marvelling at my insistence on voting, given the difficulty of doing so. Things are easier for her here.

When to leave, and when to return?

I think of the regular rush of peak-hour commuters and feel queasy. I once spent two of the four hours on the way to New York with my legs between my opposite number's, our knees interlaced in an alternating pattern, a continuing rhythm running from the aisle seats to our shared window. The first train does not worry me. It is the second, the Metro-North out of New Haven, a train of suits, hoodies, prep school uniforms, and Yankees hats. It passes through a town that made it to the national newspapers in March for a 'super-spreader' event: one birthday party, fifty guests, a visitor from Johannesburg, twenty positive test results. I see all the people waiting on the platforms as the train slides into each station, like so many vectors pointing inexorably towards me.

I decide to leave in the late morning. I have a video call at three, and the train will arrive at Grand Central ten minutes before that. I have ten minutes to look up, to observe the queue for the exit, positioning myself as far apart from everyone else as possible (six feet is surely too much to ask), to wait for the long tone of the single sliding door opening, emerging from the fluorescence of the tunnels into—what? how many other people like me?—before looking for a place, reasonably quiet, reasonably isolated, where I can log on to talk about work as if I were at home, like the others on the call, like we are all, here, still being advised to. Maybe it will be a clear day, and maybe I will take the call outside. They tell us that being outdoors reduces transmission rates by a factor of twenty. At four, I walk the six blocks to the consulate, and wait in line to vote. My train back to New Haven leaves at eight. The last leg, from New Haven to Hartford, departs at eleven.

In two days, I will leave the house to vote. I leave at eleven in the morning, and return at midnight.

We drove, just past dusk, up the mountain road
to a clearing to look in the north sky for the comet
Neowise. Comet, an icy small celestial body that when passing
close to the Sun, warms and begins to change. We drove,
on our kids' ninth birthday, up a mountain, to look
near the horizon toward the north for a comma in the sky.
We waited for a puncture of darkness. The air temperature
dropped. There was a small icy body that formed
between us as the kids fell asleep down the windy road.
We drove. It was dark. Small icy bodies. Neo, new, new year
not as in the sun. We went down. The solar winds
did not reach. Comma turned to period...

Hidden Meadows Drive

Nan Ring

Today I brought food to my mother, 93,
where her doctor won't let me stay for more than half an hour,
masked up, sitting far apart,
thinking, will I get to hug her again before she is gone?
I make
small talk,
unpack the groceries,
and stand behind her
to gingerly tie the new mask on her that I ordered hand-sewn
so she can still wear her hearing aids.
Startled again by the smallness and fragility of her skull
peeking through
the soft and milk white hair,
I make a bow,
pull just a little more,
to be sure
then apologize
at the gasped "Oh Nan!"
Through the "Watercolor Flower" pattern,
her voice, gently muffled,
saying,
Thank you. This is wonderful.

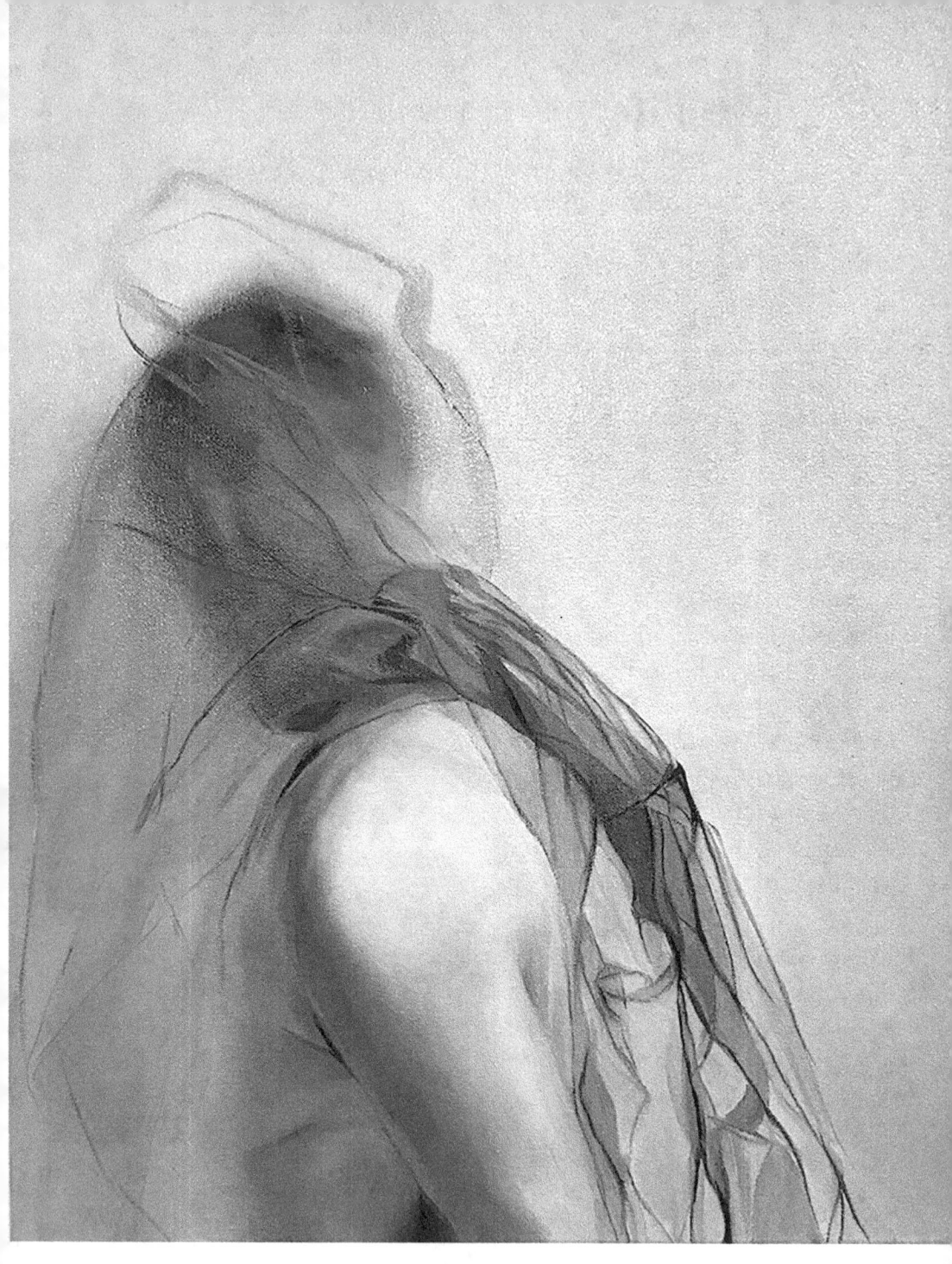

L: Nan Ring, *Letitia in Veil 3*, oil on canvas, 12″ x 12″, 2019
R: Nan Ring, *Max in Veil*, oil on canvas, 24″ x 18″, 2019

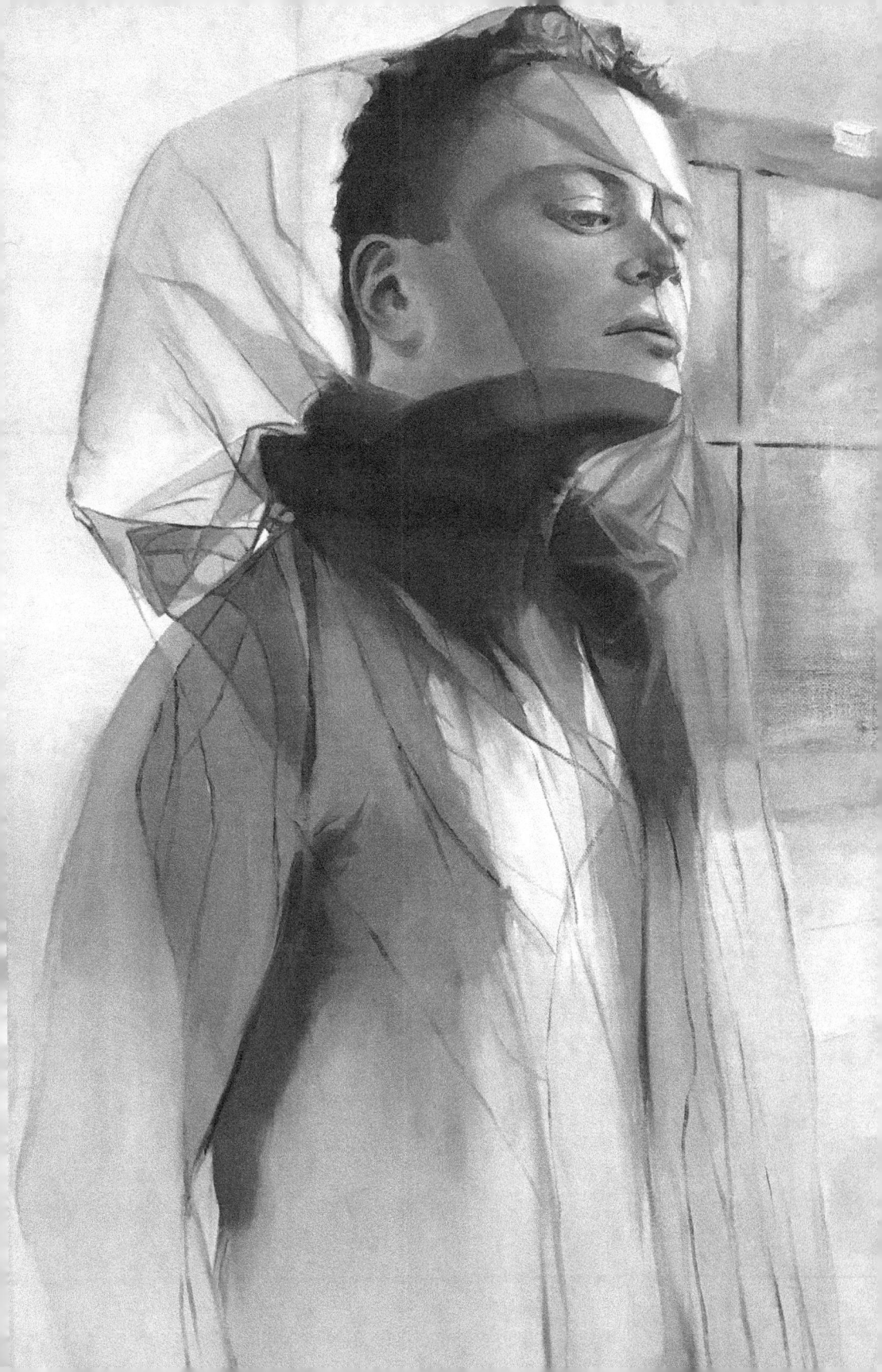

Frida Foberg, *White*, paper relief, 20" x 24", 2020

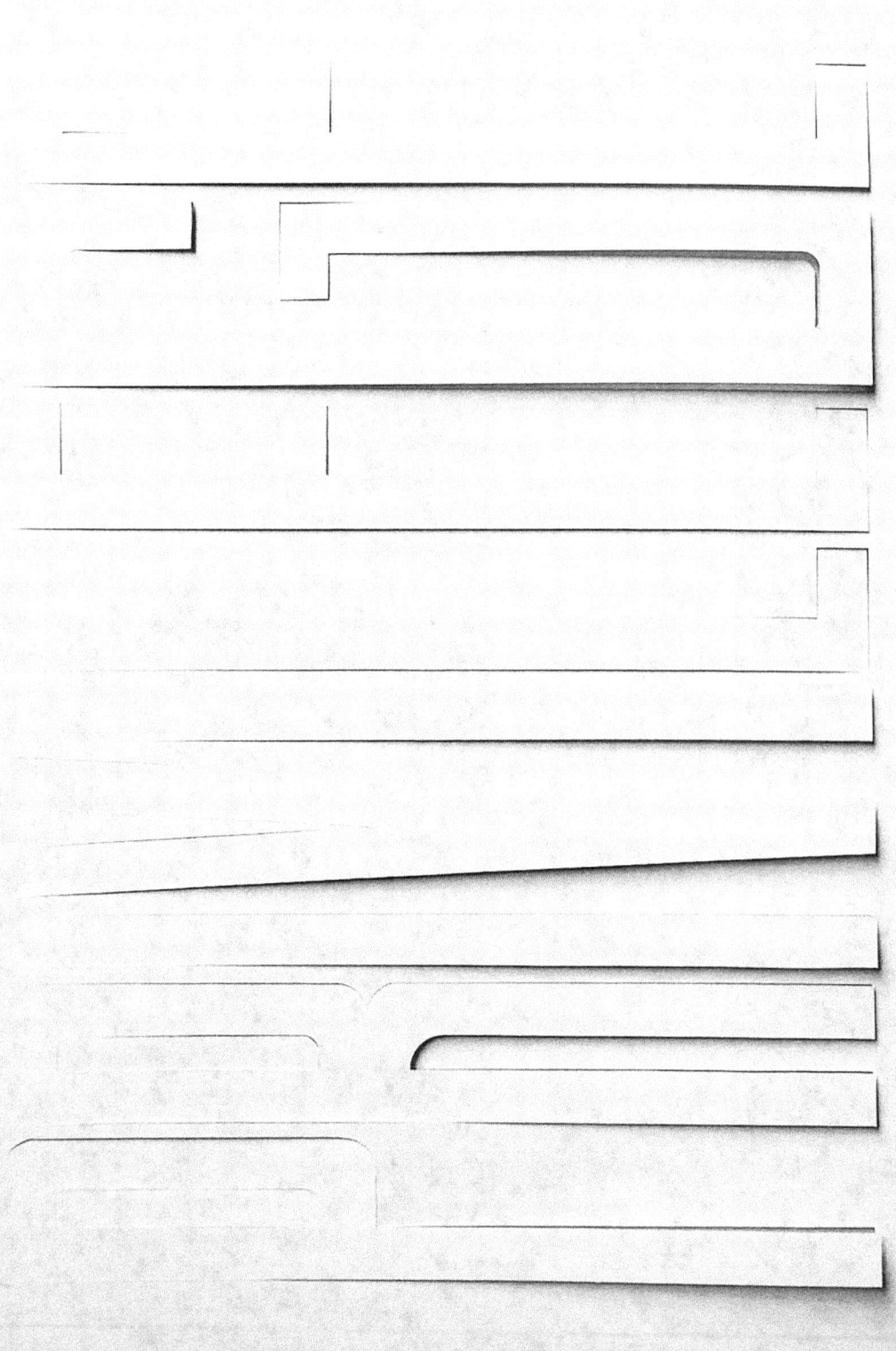

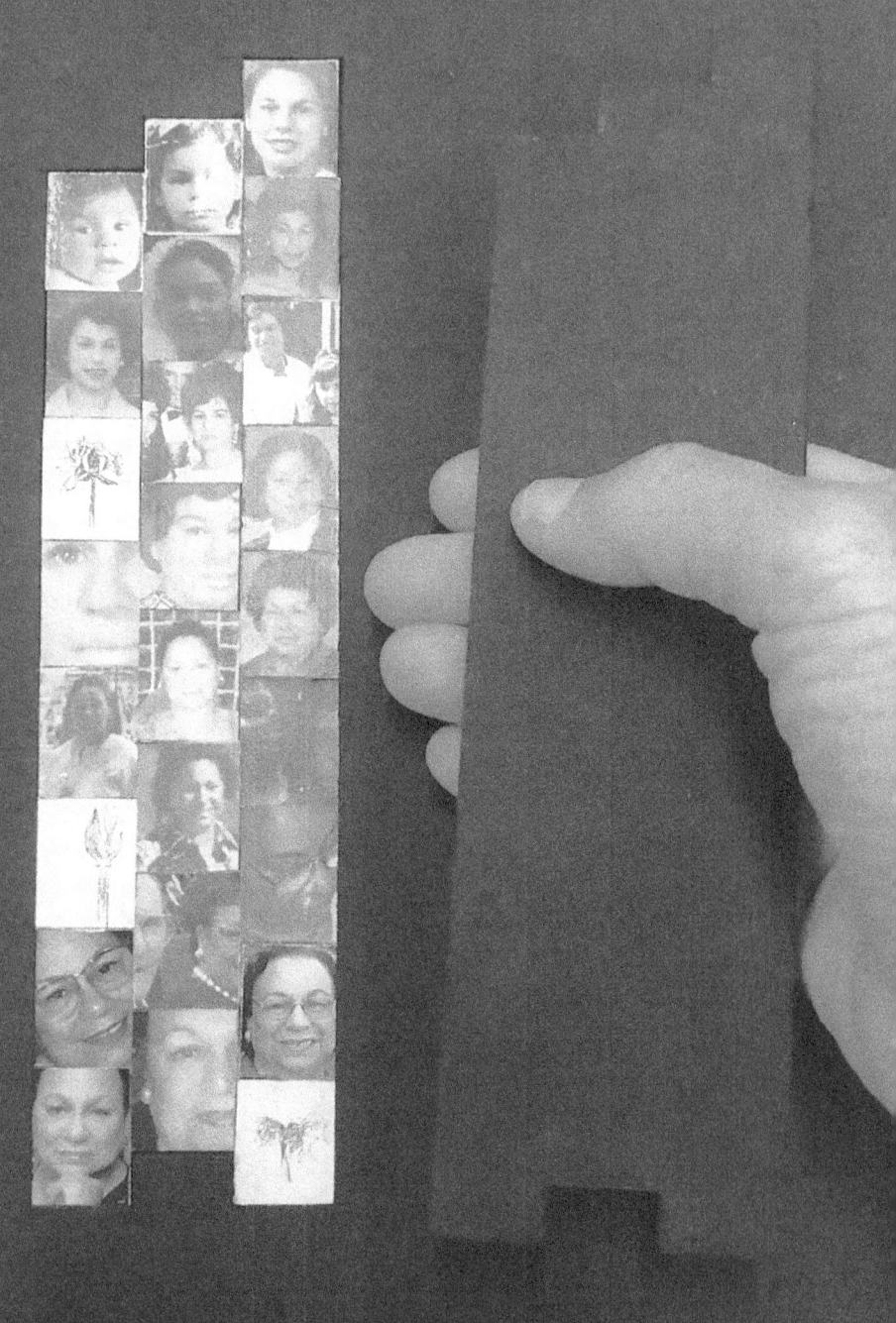

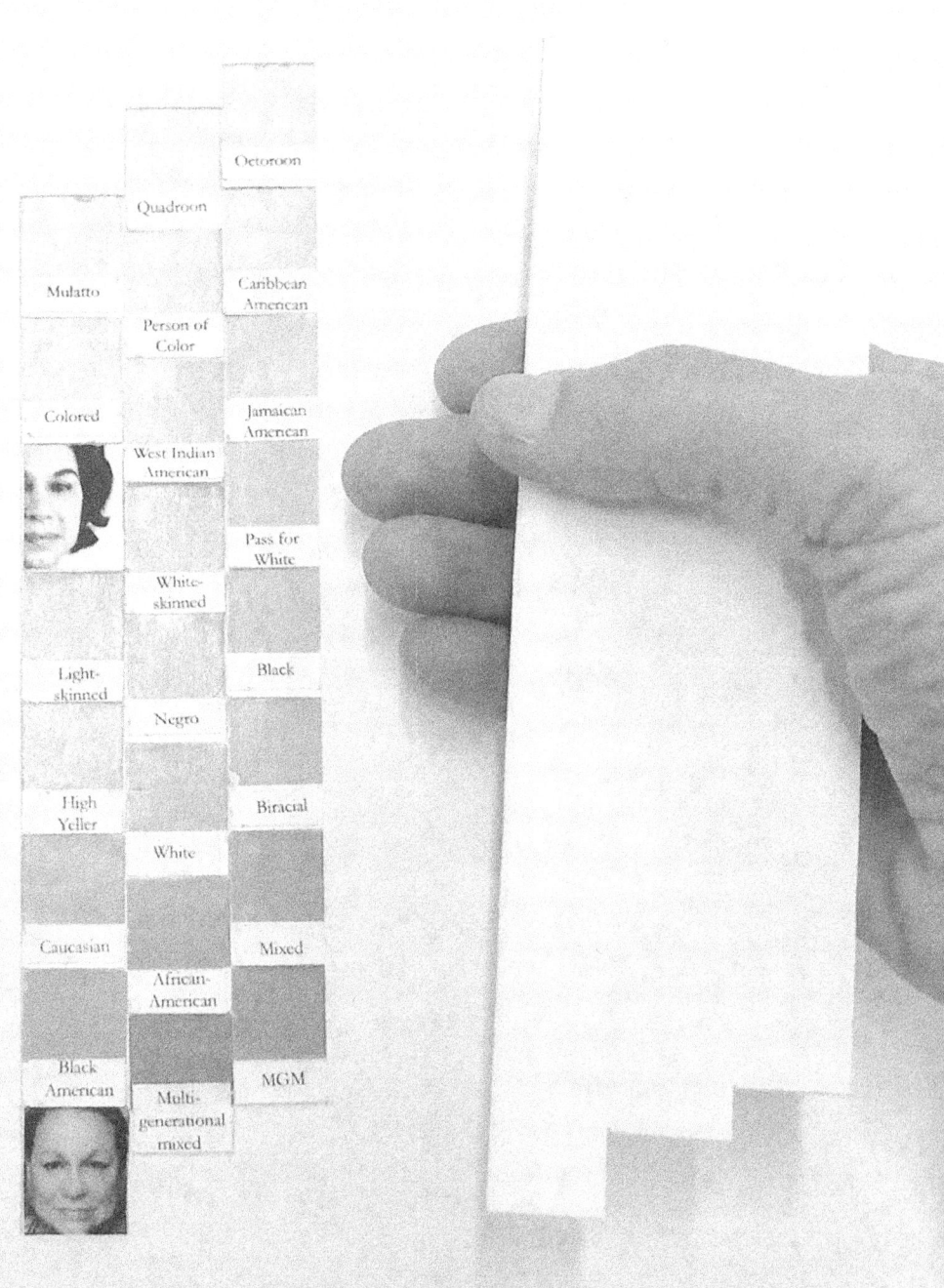

Meditation: Inter-Eruption

Becky Vartabedian

It is June 2020. BLACK LIVES MATTER is emblazoned in street-sized letters on Fifth Avenue in New York City; outside the Contra Costa County courthouse in Martinez, California and other small towns across the country; on 16th Street in Washington DC.

> JANE BENNETT: "Politics, as (Jacques) Rancière frames it, consists not in acts that preserve a political order or respond to already articulated problems, but is 'the name of a singular disruption of this order of distribution of bodies'." [1]

It is Friday, June 12, 2020. Broadway cuts through the heart of Colorado's political district, running south with the City and County of Denver building on the West side and the State Capitol on the East side. On the street in the block between Colfax Avenue and 14th Avenue, there is a mural that reads **BLACK LIVES MATTER: REMEMBER THIS TIME.**

> Rancière and other theorists of the singular disruption (or the event) work from longitudinal assumptions about history and its unfoldings, suggesting that bodies have a tendency to settle, get distributed. The settling, the distributing, is reinforced by the *polis*, the political apparatus, in 2020 the police. The *polis* has the force and power of identifying, naming, and distributing bodies: protestors, rioters, peaceful, violent. The *polis* creates and enforces dominant discursive practices. In our time, in this present historical unfolding, it has been the case that the *polis* says and shows whose lives matter.

It is Thursday, May 28. Protesters have gathered in downtown Denver–on Broadway and around the State Capitol–to protest the murder of George Floyd at the hands of Minneapolis Police. Protesters are shunted to the outer lanes of Broadway and to the sidewalk while Denver Police officers drive down the street in cars and hanging off the outside of cars, shooting non-lethal rounds, using flash-bang grenades, and tear gas to disperse protestors and reporters. The violence against reporters is especially well-documented, as they are–as is practice–clearly marked. Earlier in the evening, a civilian car charged down Broadway toward a crowd of protestors, and when it didn't meet its target, turned left across two lanes of traffic to hit a few people. Caught on video. Two days later the city will initiate a curfew; all bodies off the streets at 9pm. The news captures the *or else* implied in the Public Safety Notice that blares on all phones across the city limits.

> Periodic disruptions expose the settledness deployed by the *polis* and should

---

1   Jane Bennett, *Vibrant Matter: A Political Ecology of Things* (Durham, NC: Duke University Press, 2010), 105; quoting Jacques Rancière, *Disagreement ≠ Politics and Philosophy*, trans. Julie Rose (Minneapolis, MN: University of Minnesota Press, 1999), 99.

force a reorganization of bodies, ideas. Politics *breaks*, rather than unifies and regulates; it *inter-erupts*, per Bennett, the "coherence" of a public, *fragmenting* a sedimented order of things. Before the reorganization, though, Rancière identifies a *demos* at work that Bennet defines as "a potentially disruptive human force that exists within (though is not recognized by) the public."[2]

The *demos* is traditionally understood to be the people comprising a particular community. The *demos* is not the *polis*. The *demos* wedges a space between settledness and reorganization, "'a polemical scene' within which what was formerly heard as noise by powerful persons begins to sound to them like 'argumentative utterances'."[3] In the transformation from noise to argument, the *demos* communicates "the equality of speaking beings," revealing to everyone that "there is no natural principle of domination by one person over another."[4] The voice of the *demos* undermines the prevailing political order. As Bennett explains, "For Rancière, then, the political act consists in the exclamatory interjection of affective bodies as they enter a preexisting public, or, rather, as they reveal that they have been there all along as an unaccounted-for part."[5]

It is June 28, a Saturday. Several thousand people arrive to the designated spot in Aurora, Colorado. Some of them carry violins, all have arrived to attend the vigil for Elijah McClain, who died of a heart attack in police custody a year earlier. It will emerge that the police used an excessive dose of Ketamine to sedate McClain. Aurora, Colorado's Police department–suddenly visible on account of the gaze shifting away from Minneapolis and to Aurora, the agonized voice of Sheneen McClain finally cutting through–disperse the peaceful violin vigil wearing riot gear, using pepper spray and tear gas on the nonviolent participants, protestors playing violins. The violinists have been here all along. Elijah was a violinist. Elijah was black. Elijah was here all along. We are now accounting–slow, agonizingly slow in our accounting–for this unaccounted-for part.

In early August, members of this department will make the news again for a terrifying and unlawful traffic stop of four young black women, ranging from age 12 to age 17. The police force the young women and girls to lie on their stomachs; one of them is heard calling for her mother.

Bennett adds a editorializing remark concerning John Dewey, whose notion of the public she discussed in the previous section of her work: "Rancière would be

---

2   Bennett, 104-105.

3   Bennett, 105; quoting Rancière and Panagia, "Dissenting Worlds: A Conversation with Jacques Rancière," Diacritics 30:2 (2000), 125.

4   Rancière, *Disagreement*, pp. 33 and 79; quoted in Bennett, 105.

5   Bennett, 105.

helped here, I think, were he to adopt Dewey's insight about multiple, coexisting publics, rather than to speak of a single *demos* with an overt and a latent set of members."[6] But even in Bennett's parenthetical there's a problem of communication, simply because what our present time reveals is that in the presence of multiple, coexisting publics there aren't available notions for *hearing* the voices brought to the fore, which compete with modes by which we actively suppress these activist inter-eruptions by choice of echo chamber, by losing a grip on the truth for the purposes of wielding power, by drowning them out with layers and layers of noise *purposefully*, so that they *cannot be heard*.

Tear gas.

Flash bangs.

Riot gear and armored vehicles, non-lethal rounds that silence by blinding.

In St. Louis, in a viral moment made for our present historical unfolding, a white couple emerges from their palatial residence, barefoot and brandishing guns at protestors just passing through the neighborhood.

Rancière's account would suggest that once a *demos* inter-erupts into a public the space it creates makes hearing possible. But who is it among the public that *legitimates* this hearing? At least Bennett suggests that the voices speak in ways that are legible to a public that has previously ignored them.

Why is it that George Floyd's death–so needless and casual in its extreme violence–is the catalyzing inter-eruption, when voices demanding that black lives matter have been sounding for far longer than now? Elijah McClain speaks a year after his killing, in the sound of violins and children crying for their mother. Sheneen McClain, Elijah's mother, has been calling for justice in all this time. The question of legitimate hearing–can we hear the *demos* speak?–is why the mural on Broadway in Denver demands we **REMEMBER THIS TIME**. Remember the disruption, re-order the bodies and the ideas and the discourses and the apparatus.

Politics is the between-space, the cracks, the *demos* on the asphalt, its feet maintained now by paint. Paint that will fade in 30-45 days now that the protests have faded from immediate view.

Remember this time.

Justice for Elijah McClain.

---

6   Bennett, 105.

Grit & Dripping

June Lucarotti

And here, in this time of the virus, everything has blurred together. It has actually been my dream come true to transcend borders. To transpose and integrate our villages. To have the people be the geography. Suddenly, Costa Rica is grit and Colorado is dripping. San Francisco is bursting, pregnant. Ready. Suddenly Glide church hymns overlay Soul Tree sanskrit breath and *mensaje de Elmer sobre la salud en* the village. It all happens in the same day and we are blurred. An impressionist painting. It is said by therapists that enmeshment is negative. We need boundaries. We can't bleed into one another. But are we sure? Isn't there some beauty in bleeding into one another? Knowing that our true nature lies in the tongue and saliva of another. Knowing the collective ocean that we will go back to, now? I will be blurring the lines. I will be watching it all drip into each other. And I will allow myself to throw my head back, mouth wide open and pinched at the creases, sparkle in my eye, and laugh. It is supposed to be this way. I don't know why or how, but I do believe it is all supposed to be this way. We are on the right path. We just have to hold on.

can you group them

as often happens subconsciously

where they are breaking

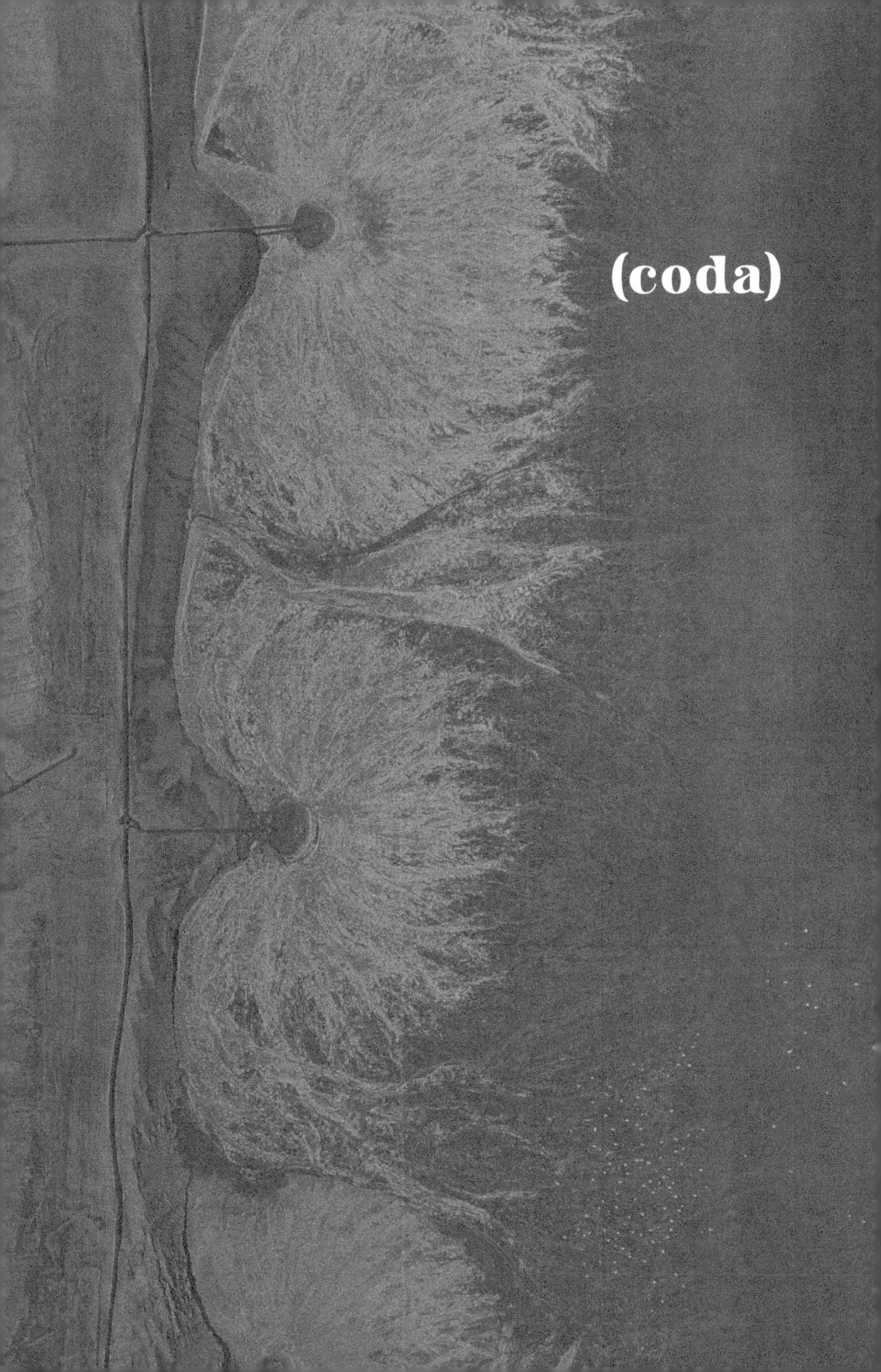

(coda)

Petalless/Petalous

Andrew Helton

1. Everything that is close to me is closed to me. Or was it
   the other way. Near is nearly. Nay is nigh. Beside besides.

2. To spiral is both an act of creation and destruction. Doing
   and undoing. The changing of a path in which the only two
   constants are beginning and end with no interaction inbetween.
   Inside is different than in-between.

3. The way hold will never satisfy held. The way indifferent
   and in-between are the same. Witness and witnessed.

4. I am bound to be let. A room. A place. Let down. To be
   cleaved. Let up. I am nobody. Who are you?

Listen, the Bees Still Hum

Ginger Teppner

We veneer civilization by doing unkind things in a kind way.

—George Bernard Shaw

The liberty of the individual is no gift of civilization. It was greatest before there was any civilization.

—Sigmund Freud

> How the universe inside of my ribcage wants to splash free. How my cicada cells want to sing. How every neuron has a sister star in the sky—the same sky contained in my spleen. If I stand in one spot long enough will the trees recognize me? If I stand in one spot long enough will my eyes adjust to the light that existed before language told me what I can or cannot see? If I stand in one place long enough will I slip past metaphor and simile and cadence and rhyme and recognize myself—*as a ribbon as a vein as a current as a thorn as a wing   as a letter as a howl as a speck   as dust   as dust as dust?*

We can always be more, or less, isolated by how much we focus on isolated fragments of time, as if much of life isn't spent enduring. The privilege inherent in the assumption that civilization is owed to us and the degree to which ecology and economy can be weaponized are problems born of our refusals to accept the limitedness of words and the potential continuity of empathy, gratitude, and the beauty in all the little broken things—the unanswerable questions.

If before there was language, there was poetry, pure expression of experience—experience steeped in the unanswerable questions that span from the beginning of no time to the end of no time, our first word uttered: fear. It must have been, since all the words that followed were built to accomplish the impossible. To name the things. To erase the distance between. To hide our terror— an unfortunate byproduct of curious human minds with incredible imaginations that desire to bend the wide wild world into predictable outcomes.

> (As a human writer, I sense the majestic force of nature growing in my front yard is no more a "tree" than I am or as much of a tree as I am, depending on my mood. I and know and the and majestic and force and of and nature are, too, only words, words we have collectively agreed to agree upon, but, still, I try to get as close to the thing I'm naming as possible because this is how I (we) navigate the world.)

In this way, like civilization, language was sold to us as comfort. A warm blanket to prevent chill, a veil of superiority to justify, proof for assumption, validation for struggle, illusion to distract, evidence of meaning.

But also, expression of beauty. In this way separation was the price we were willing to pay to articulate tree and sky and bee and hawk. To be able to comment on the weather, the flavor and texture of the rain, how the earth smells like a body in various stages of composition and decomposition. And the more abstract: love and pain and desire and jealousy and war. How we crave the words to sling as weapons. You are that. I am this. Our exodus from Eden. To make it easier to perceive and devour. Patterns, manifest over and over, reverberate in a familiar tone. Like a memory on the tip of your tongue. That you know that you know but can't quite remember.

We are archaic-barbaric. The power of intention made manifest through symbols. How we pretend the words are what make us special— better than. Were we willing to leave well enough alone, to scramble and frolic along the unnamed river banks, to sleep nestled, nested like owls without having to taste the name owl as it crosses our lips, perhaps the notion of boundaries would not have stuck? Maybe we would still remember the joy of being outside outside—of having our genius exposed— freedom from, for, of, beyond.

In the place of judgement—wickedness was there/In the place of justice—wickedness was there. Maybe Ecclesiastes got it right. Everything is meaningless. We come from dust and return to dust. *Whatever is has already been, and what will be has been before.* Tear down your walled civilizations, strip off your coat of words, and stand naked in this wild experience. Literally and symbolically burn it all down, or at the very least give it your best shot. Go ahead, keep trying to get closer and closer to the right name. You will fail time and time again, and you will keep trying. This is your life's work. From this rupture between being and knowing we spend life collecting crates of bicycles and doors swung ponderously open. *Below the coccoloba uvifera listen, the bees still hum.*

About the Authors

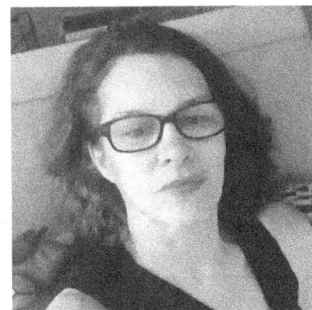

University Park, MD
lesliebernsstudio.com

Leslie Berns is a Senior Lecturer in Art at the University of Maryland. She told us more than once that writing is not her most intuitive language, but the images and words she shared—particularly her deep and joyous relationship with plant matter—betray that she intuits the world in lush detail, and can express these intuitions with writing as strongly as with her visual artistry. Maybe it is because of her work across sculpture, film, and paper that her way of seeing is so textural. She shows us the details in sparseness and abundance. She invites us in. NL

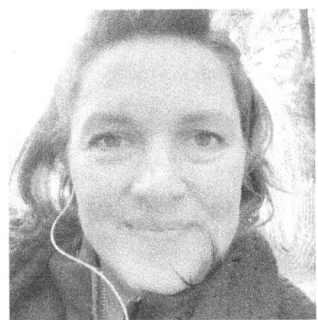

Dana Brinson

Hillsborough NC
consultingbetwixt.com

Dana owns consultingbetwixt. com and partners with people through change and dying.

Her texts are woven through with narrative, mysteries and Celtic lore. She is a gardener nurturing life from subterranean darkness to branches set against southern skies. A lover of trees. Motherline traced back to great great great great great greats, traced through caves, through tears, through water, through form, through snapshots and secrets, osprey and tides and rivermen, and land let go. She is a teacher of letting go, navigator of change. A witch conjuring words and opening doors. AM

Evan Burgess

New York NY
Instagram: @an_iceburg

Evan Burgess is considerate. He is especially mindful of the strength and fragility inherent in the language of what we choose to preserve. In his work questions echo: What are we accumulating? And what of the things that don't stand over time? His imagination is contagious and his compulsion to archive is more than merely nostalgic. Yes, he is a cartographer leaving a trail of pebbles for future anthropologists, but he also graciously remembers to always leave a trace of breadcrumbs for the birds. GT

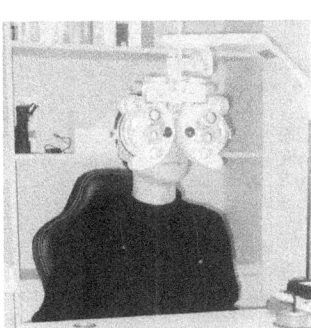

Tielin Ding

New York NY
Instagram: @mr.something0110

Born in 1996 in Chongqing, China. Tielin Ding is an an urban flaneur, observer and interdisciplinary artist based in NYC whose diverse practice involves working with playful objects, indeterminate traces and movements to create durational performative actions. His application of the methodology of "Mapping" and "Walking as Research Practice" gives him more opportunity to reflect on invisible systems within different sites and spaces. He received a Bachelor of Engineering in civil engineering from Beijing University of Civil Engineering and Architecture in 2018 and is now studying for an MFA degree in Photography and Related Media at Parsons School of Design. His works have been exhibited in Feldfuenf in Berlin, Germany; in Cologne collabaration with Reclaim Award, Germany; Photographic Center Northwest in Seattle, USA; Wilgus Gallery in Baltimore, USA; UCCA and ThreeShadows in Beijing, China; and Polar Bear Gallery in Shanghai, China.

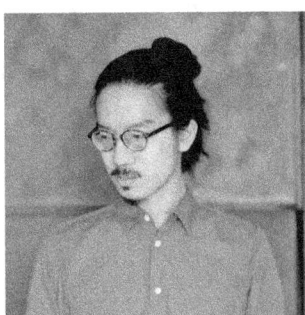

Shou Jie Eng

New Haven CT | shoujie.net

Shou Jie joined *The Earth Of* introductory Zoom meeting July 6, 2020 by phone from an outdoor public space in Manhattan. Masked, in a global pandemic, he travelled that day by train and bus from Hartford to New Haven to New York City to cast his absentee ballot in Singapore's election. Both his drawings and writings are accumulations of perceptions of space, meaningful transparent layers arrived at through a deeply empathetic, imaginative, analytical process. A designer at Left Field Projects, "an independent studio practice involved in the production of writing, research, and design at the architectural and urban scales", Shou Jie Eng studied architecture at the Rhode Island School of Design and law at the London School of Economics and Political Science. LB

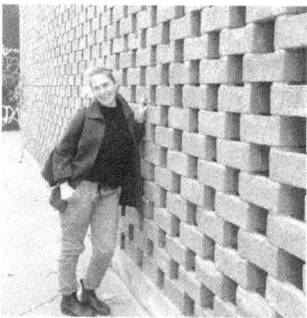

Frida Foberg
Averill Park NY | fridafoberg.com

Frida Foberg was associate director of Arts Letters & Numbers. Frida is instrumental in many things. She has been helping to facilitate this program as well as hundreds of others over the past years. But beyond bringing us together, Frida has also been joining us in struggling with the questions and the words and the life that we've been experiencing in this workshop. I know that place, of being always a little bit on the outside, and a little bit on the inside. I have an enormous respect for the sensitivity that Frida brings to her work. I've seen the hundreds of times that she folds everyone around her into the work that she does. And

it is also a joy to see Frida figure out how to carve out a place for herself. EB

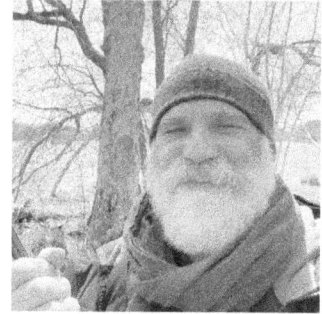

David Gersten
Averill Park NY
artslettersandnumbers.com

David Gersten is the founding director of Arts Letters & Numbers. David Gersten is a master time mechanic, an architect seduced by poetry, a liberator, an educator, and an alchemist. His work translates the conditional pause born of rupture into a multi- disciplinary language of bone and breath and breeze, an unparalleled vernacular meant to bridge the inside and outside space that completes us. Suspended in the ripple and flutter of his intense observation, fragments blossom into tides. GT

Andrew Helton
Chinook WA

Andrew Helton is precise. This precision is not fragile. Its strength is born of rigorous closeness. Every endeavor he initiates is created with intention and thorough engagement. He is not afraid of exertion or difficulty; in fact, he relishes the uncomfortable challenges necessary for growth. Because of this, no question is left unexplored, whether he is training for a powerlifting competition, printmaking, editing a manuscript, creating a life with his equally talented wife, or writing poetry.

His poetic subtleties are the elemental stuff the Earth is made of: rooted in equal parts encyclopedic knowledge and profound compassion. His keen sensitivity, intuition, and imagination direct him time and again towards the inexpressible, that which lies beyond words. His integrity drives him, not only to personally experience all of everything but to create a new space for the rest of us to inhabit as well, as witness and witnessed, and we are better for it. GT

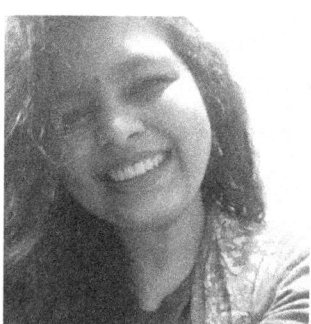

Darshita Jain
Chicago IL

Darshita Jain is a Chicago-based journalist, critic, and performance poet. She recently completed a Master's Degree in New Arts Journalism at the School of the Art Institute of Chicago. Her poem "There is a Chorus Line Somewhere in this Poem" was published at 433 Magazine in the last week of our work together. Darshita is the cofounder of POVERA, the first spoken word poetry organization in Ahmedabad, India. Darshita's voice and words are breath, music, and life. BV

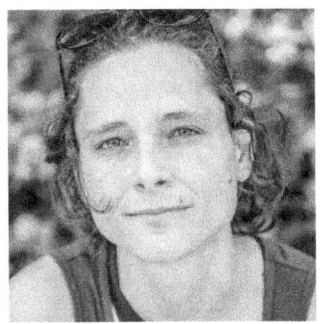

Annie Jacobs
Troy NY

You wish that some people were more aware, more gentle in the observance of daily life and themselves. Annie's work–rich in reflective pause moments, reads like talking to a close friend. Bittersweet conclusions on past and present. Room for growth. Mostly, I think, we understand each other's yearn for comfort and clutch to the moments that make us feel most present. Annie writes, draws, and makes collages to express the many forms of life, and places on earth, she has been lucky to interact with. She works in the environmental field, volunteers on local farms, and is most at home in nature and with animals. AM

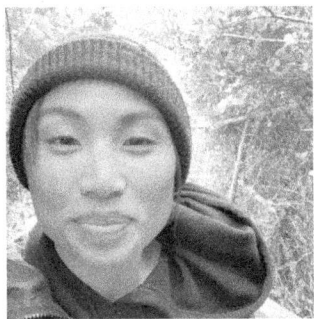

Nicole Le
San Diego CA

Nicole Le is a writer whose everyday life involves intricate detail and keen observation. She works as a scientific researcher at UC San Diego, and she absorbs her environment: a coastal desert with "careening valleys and falcons and irrepressible hordes of rabbits and suburbia and the packing in of lizards and sparrows and coyotes and people and dogs and snakes." At Oberlin College, she was a triple major - biology, neuroscience, and literature. Her writing is articulated with a precision that examines life the way a doctor would. And, while writing about the physical world seems to come easily to her, with almost a naturalist's view, she is not afraid to divulge her inner world, rich with the human experience. Any story comes through with her decisive and honest voice. Nicole is an emerging writer to follow. Her stories are going somewhere that I would hate to miss out on; we should all be watching. AJ

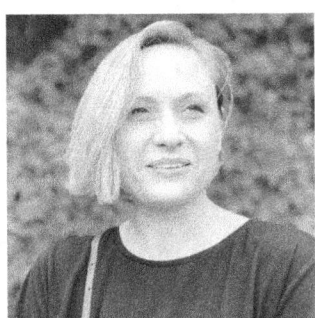

Christine Lorenz
Pittsburgh PA | cmlorenz.com

Christine Lorenz turned the projects from *The Earth Of* into this book. Christine uses photography to examine the ordinary, overlooked, disposable, and forgotten. She earned her MFA at the University of California, Santa Barbara, and BA at Ohio State University. Her photographs have been seen at photo-eye gallery in Santa Fe, in Pittsburgh galleries, and elsewhere across the United States and Europe. Online, her work has been featured by Vice, Photolucida, Rogue Agent, Magenta Foundation and Humble Arts. She lives with her family in Pittsburgh, PA, where she teaches visual culture at Duquesne University and art writing at Point Park University.

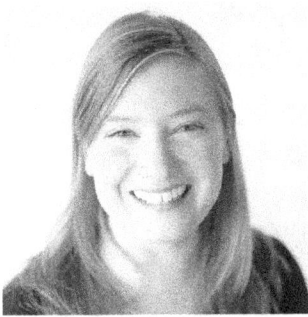

June Lucarotti
CO | volasessions.com

June Lucarotti, a master of words and "collective oceans," is the birth mother of Birth Your Book, a book coaching course infused with yoga recovery and creative writing. A private editing eye, youth camp and retreat empowerer, a Soul tree certified transcender of boundaries, an allower of head-thrown-back-sparkle-in-the-eye laughter, June is also on a search for "busy joy." You can often find her following "rolling clouds," workshopping meditation and writing, and leading in Spanish as well as English. UC Berkeley bestowed upon her a BA in Social Welfare, and Buddhist inspired Naropa University conferred upon her an MFA in writing and poetics. She is currently trying to learn to love snakes. NR

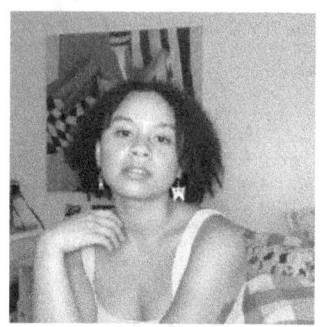

Annisia Martinez
Queens NY | annisiamartinez.net

Annisia is a poet of clarity, vulner-ability, and warmth. Her poems are carefully observed, without the entanglements of delusion or cynicism. They read, at times, like a practice of holding onto the earth by patiently naming things that are real, what is present to the hand, and to the heart: what matters. They have no use for embellishment or elaboration. Her lines are clean as a stone thrown into still water. The sound creates a vivid image: a particular depth, a particular weight; sensed, not described. The circles expand precisely, vanish quickly, and the moment is gone. CL

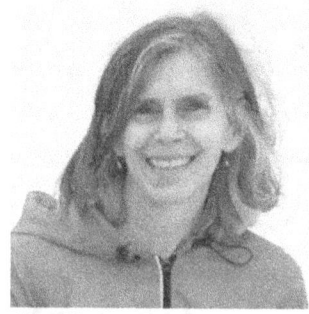

Alice Momm
New York NY | alicemomm.com

Alice Momm is a New York City based artist whose work has been inspired both by her immersion in and longing for nature. Her ephemeral and sculptural works have been exhibited at venues such as Wave Hill in the Bronx, Islip Art Museum in East Islip, NY, Ham-bidge Center in Rabun Gap, GA, The Arsenal Gallery, NYC, and the Visual Arts Center of New Jersey. She has participated in many artist residencies includ-ing I-Park in East Haddam, CT, Hambidge Center, Stone Quarry Hill Art Park, and Arts, Letters & Numbers. Momm holds an MFA from the University of Southern California and a BFA from the University of Massachusetts, Amherst. In addition to her work as an artist, Momm is a curator specializing in art in health care settings.

Alice Momm is a poet who instantly transports us from a gritty city landscape to alliga-tors and sunburns to wet moss underfoot and a little velvet tear. Her poetry scoops us up from our daily dramas, into a kind of lullaby, always awaiting the next moment of peace, and the next bubbling of magic. JL

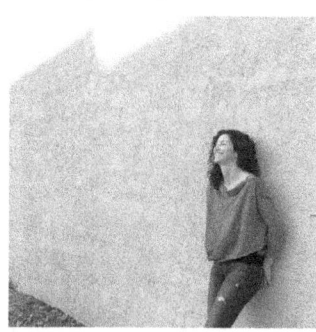

Robin Mullery
San Francisco Bay Area CA
robinmullery.art

Robin Mullery is a sculptor, a writer, and a therapist, who works with concrete and do es beautiful work with concrete language. In the first week, she wrote something that caught the eye. She said, "thank you for holding it all softly," which says so much about her work. "Thank you" is about the gratitude that she brings to the work, which she does "softly"—hers is a work of heavy things treated softly, a work of cracks and ruptures through which light cannot help but cross, a work of darkness so that you see the light. And through it all, "holding"—the insistent, ineffable pressure of a sculptor's hands. SE

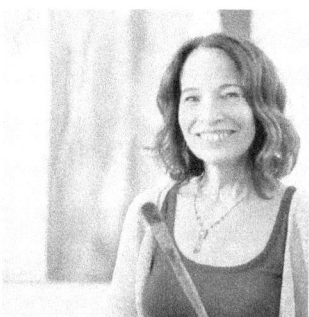

Nan Ring
West Orange NJ |
nanringstudio.com

Nan Ring is a visual artist and author who has been the re-cipient of numerous grants and awards for her fine art such as a NEA Fellowship Award in Works on Paper, and a NYFA Artists' Fellowship Award in Drawing. She has been awarded summer artist-in-residence studios at Virginia Center for Creative Arts, Hambidge Center, GA, Ucross Foundation, Wyoming, Brush Creek Foundation, Wyoming, chaNorth, New York, Ipark,, Con-necticut, Djerrassi and the Mon-talvo Center for the Arts, both in California, Soaring Gardens, Pa., and The Vermont Studio Center. Her fine art has been exhib-ited nationally and is included in public collections such as Prudential Insurance, Coca Cola, Phillip Morris, and others.

Ring is the author of *Walking On Walnuts*, Bantam, 1996 (national media, regional bestseller.) She has appeared on many television and radio shows and lectured at the Smithsonian Institute, Washington D.C. Her writing has appeared in the Newark Star Ledger, Newsday, and The New York Times Magazine, including others. Ring earned her MFA from The University of the Arts, Philadelphia, Pa and her BFA from Syracuse University School of Visual and Performing Arts. A transplanted Manhattanite, she lives in northern New Jersey, and is the proud mother of a 22-year-old son, a musician based in Memphis.

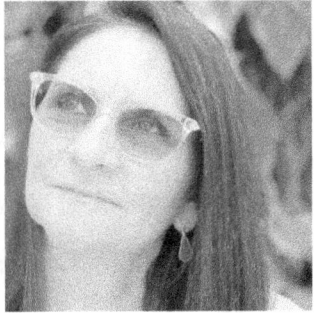

Ginger Teppner
Winter Haven FL | gingerteppner.com

Ginger Teppner originated and directed *The Earth of.* As a poet, Ginger Teppner is an architect, a textile weaver, a master builder of places where there had once only been sensation and longing. Her propensity for evolving the world into nouns creates spaces that can only exist in language— a world where the thoughts and feelings we cannot express can live and, for a moment, we are free of the pain of the limits of our bodies. Somehow, these spaces do not only exist on the page or in her voice. She embodies them as a teacher, as a mother, and as a friend. To know her is to be held entirely and with the same gentleness and consideration as the gorgeous language she creates.

Entering Ginger's work is like waking up in a field of clothes hung out to dry. As you move you feel the sharpness of the lemon-yellow sun graze the back of your neck between damp sheets, you smell the bloom of a lilac, you hear the flutter and screech of birds looking for food before an evening rain comes, telling you an evening rain is coming. You feel the pain of the memory. Not nostalgia. Not a memory of the past. A memory that is and was here now with you and the pain is knowing that it can somehow only live in this place and you will have to leave. And she is the linen—blocking your view, forcing you to feel your way, occasionally reaching up in the breeze to brush your cheek. She is the movement in the fracture. AH

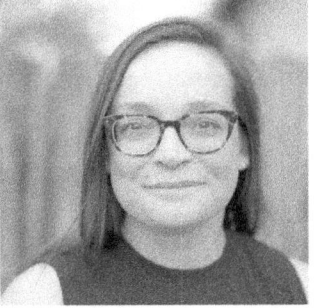

Becky Vartabedian
Denver CO
beckyvartabedian.substack.com

Becky Vartabedian is Associate Professor of Philosophy at Regis University in Denver, Colorado. Her research interests are in contemporary Continental philosophy. Becky thinks that philosophy is at its best when everyone can share in its deep well of resources for our individual lives and lives lived in community. In the coming year, she will be working on a large project about hospitality and urban life. She weaves philosopher's insights with current moments, seeking ever to use her training to help herself and others Live Deliberately and to Live Well. She is sometimes possessed by the ghosts of crash-and-smash

and "just enough" from her patriline. She loves to lift heavy objects and to watch, astonished, as her husband moves like water. And she enjoys her two pups, one older—the teacher, one younger—the apprentice. Becky's writing is at once erudite and inviting, abrupt and tender and I know you will enjoy what she has to share. DB

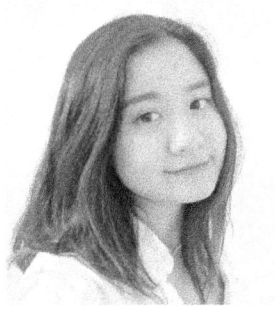

Jisu Yang
Providence RI

Jisu Yang is currently a student of architecture and design at Rhode Island School of Design. She works across disciplines and from what I have had the privilege to observe, she is a poet of the minute and mutation. She observes everything from nature to nurture, in lines and angles and what emerges are deeply humbling human depictions. She is so quiet, so calm, but the way she looks at the world is so sharp, I can't wait to explore what emerges out of her and we get to interact with the way she looks at the world around her. DJ

Arts Letters & Numbers is a non-profit arts and education organization dedicated to fostering creative exchanges across a broad range of disciplines including architecture, visual arts, theatre arts, film, music, humanities, sciences, and social sciences. Operating globally, regionally and locally, Arts Letters & Numbers seeks to bring together voices of diverse backgrounds, practices and ages. It conducts programs in educational and cultural institutions worldwide, and runs interdisciplinary artist-in-residence programs, as well as educational workshops, sessions, exhibitions and events, in their Averill Park, NY campus. Arts Letters & Numbers is an idea about education, about the transformation of knowledge created by bringing diverse forms of creative expression into direct proximity. The educational programs create spaces of participation, of communication, of reciprocity, for people and their works to listen to each other, to listen to the world. All of this is working towards a new vision of education that is grounded in an ethics of inclusion and embracing a great diversity of people, voices and ways of knowing.

www.ingramcontent.com/pod-product-compliance
Lightning Source LLC
Chambersburg PA
CBHW070542220526
45467CB00003B/1024